FIELDS UNSOWN

by

Catherine Harvey and Louise Monaghan

Commissioned by Attic Theatre Company.
First performed at Morden Hall Park, Surrey, on 17 September 2014.

Published by Playdead Press 2014

© Catherine Harvey and Louise Monaghan 2014

Catherine Harvey and Louise Monaghan have asserted their rights under the Copyright, Design and Patents Act, 1988, to be identified as the authors of this work.

A CIP catalogue record for this book is available from the British Library.

ISBN 978-1-910067-23-9

Caution

Printed by BPUK

Playdead Press
www.playdeadpress.com

Fields Unsown

by Catherine Harvey and Louise Monaghan

Cast (in order of appearance)

Gilliat Edward Hatfeild	**Richard Heap**
Billy Baker	**James Fletcher**
Matron Enid Woods	**Hannah Boyde**
Sergeant Alex Forbes	**Toyin Omari-Kinch**
V.A.D. Lizzie Baker	**Ffion Jolly**
Private Robby Stephens	**Rick Yale**
V.A.D. Ella Ewing Chapple	**Naomi Everson**

Production team

Director	**Louise Hill**
Designer	**Harriet de Winton**
General Manager	**Victoria Hibbs**
Stage Manager	**Danyal Shafiq**
Press and Marketing	**Chris Williams**
Consultant	**Jenny Lee**
Marketing & Research Assistant	**Kirsty Emmerson**
Publicity Design	**Roshana Rubin-Mayhew**
Production photography	**Jack Ladenburg**

Hannah Boyde | Matron Enid Woods

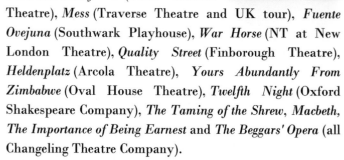

Hannah trained at Drama Studio London.

Theatre includes *Lands of Glass* (Summerhall, Edinburgh), *Dora* and *Henry V* (both Unicorn Theatre), *Mess* (Traverse Theatre and UK tour), *Fuente Ovejuna* (Southwark Playhouse), *War Horse* (NT at New London Theatre), *Quality Street* (Finborough Theatre), *Heldenplatz* (Arcola Theatre), *Yours Abundantly From Zimbabwe* (Oval House Theatre), *Twelfth Night* (Oxford Shakespeare Company), *The Taming of the Shrew, Macbeth, The Importance of Being Earnest* and *The Beggars' Opera* (all Changeling Theatre Company).

Television includes *The Last Days of Anne Boleyn* (BBC2) and *At Home With the Georgians* (BBC2).

Radio includes *Gracey & Me* (Radio 4).

Naomi Everson | V.A.D. Ella Ewing Chapple

Naomi trained at The Royal Welsh College of Music and Drama.

Theatre includes *The Radicalization of Bradley Manning,* (Edinburgh Fringe Festival).

Theatre whilst training includes *Boston Marriage, The Cherry Orchard, Picnic, Once a Catholic, Lower Depths, Anne Boleyn.*

Film includes *Testament of Youth* (BBC Films), *Delight* (Scenario Films) and *The Zero Theorem* (Media Pro Studios).

Television includes *A Poet In New York* (BBC1), *Atlantis* (Urban Myth Films for BBC1), *The Indian Doctor* (Rondo/Avatar Films for BBC2), *Shelf Stackers* (Lime Pictures for Channel 4).

James Fletcher | Billy Baker

James trained at The London Academy of Music and Dramatic Art.

Theatre includes *Love and a Bottle* (Greenwich Theatre), *Pornography* (LAMDA Linbury Studio), *Sweeney Todd* (POSK), *A Midsummer Night's Dream* (The Pleasance), *The Lightning Play* (LAMDA Linbury Studio), *Cymbeline* (Tabard Theatre) and *The Exclusion Zone* (Southwark Playhouse).

Film includes *In the Stream* (LAMDA).

Television includes *Newsnight's How to Die* (BBC), *Downton Abbey* (BBC) and *Harlots, Housewives and Heroines* (BBC).

Richard Heap | Gilliat Edward Hatfield

Theatre includes *Mansfield Park* (Theatre Royal Bury St. Edmunds and tour), *Hard Times*, (Arcadia), *Great Expectations*, *A Doll's House*, *Skylight* and *The Resistible Rise of Arturo Ui* (Library Theatre Manchester), *The Story of Vasco* (Richmond Orange Tree), *To Kill a Mockingbird* (West Yorkshire Playhouse/Birmingham Rep and tour), *The Demolition Man and Broken Glass* (Bolton Octagon), *White People and Natural Selection* (Theatre 503), *A Christmas Carol*, *The Accrington Pals*, *Under Milk Wood and Tom Thumb*, (Dukes Lancaster), *The Quiet Little Englishman and Angels in America* (Liverpool Unity), *The Winter's Tale* (Salisbury Playhouse), *Saint Joan*, *The Tempest* and *The Winter's Tale* (A&BC Theatre), *Robbers* (Tristan Bates).

Film includes *A Little Chaos, Outlanders, The Gospel of John, There's Only One Jimmy Grimble, Angel, Starfly* and *Hillsborough*.

TV includes *A Good Thief, Heartbeat, Casualty, Murphy's Law, Cold Feet, EastEnders, Coronation Street, Emmerdale, Doctors, Hollyoaks* and *Brookside*.

Ffion Jolly | V.A.D. Lizzie Baker

Ffion Jolly trained at Bristol Old Vic
Theatre School.

Theatre includes *The Energy Show*
(Science Museum Live), *Mansfield
Park* (No.1 tour), *The Girl with the
Iron Claws* (The Wrong Crowd), *Sam
Rose in the Shadows* (Tucked In), *Money Matters*
(Nabokov), *Fitzrovia Radio Hour* (No.1 Tour), *Macbeth*
(Baz Productions), *Richard II, The Comedy of Errors, A
Midsummer Night's Dream, The Tempest* (all Shakespeare
at the Tobacco Factory), *Auricular* (Theatre 503), *Othello*
(Creation Theatre Company), *The Elephant in the Room*
(Wimbledon Theatre), *Basura, Race For Paradise* (INCA,
Southwark Playhouse).

Film includes *Timedancer* (Microsoft), *All the Wars*
(Macfarlane Productions), *Dip It* (WhatHo Records),
Callum (VDP Productions), *O Romeo, Romeo...* (Paul
Purnell Films).

Radio Includes *An Unchoreographed World* (BBC Radio 4),
Romeo and Juliet (Wireless Theatre Co).

Ffion was nominated for the Ian Charleson Award for *The
Comedy of Errors* (SATTF).

Toyin Omari-Kinch | Sergeant Alex Forbes

Toyin trained at Birmingham Theatre School.

Theatre includes *At The Gates of Gaza* (Birmingham Repertory Theatre), *Marcus Da Sadist* (Jonzi D Productions), *Not Quite Gospel* (Nu Century Arts), *The Lost Happy Endings* (mac Birmingham / Red Earth Theatre), *The Day the Waters Came* (Theatre Centre), *The Flying Machine* (Unicorn Theatre) and *Circles*, (Birmingham Repertory Theatre).

Film and television credits include *The Games Men Play* (B19 Media), *The Door*, (Soap Box / Creative Partnerships) and *Doctors* (BBC).

Rick Yale | Private Robby Stephens

Rick trained at Rose Bruford College.

Theatre includes *Anne Boleyn* (Stratford Circus), *Perfect Boy* (Bargehouse), *Rocket to the Moon* (Rose Bruford), *Macbeth* (Rose Bruford), *A View from the Bridge* (Rose Bruford), *Romeo and Juliet* (The Gate Arts Centre).

Louise Monaghan | Playwright

Louise won the Papatango New Writing Festival in 2012 for her play *Pack* (Finborough Theatre). Her play *My Space* premiered at last year's 24:7 Festival in Manchester. She won a Bruntwood Prize Judges' Award for *Shadow Play* in 2011 and was a finalist for both the London Fringe Festival's Theatre Writing Award 2010 and Little Brother's Big Opportunity 2011 with her play *Aurora*. Louise participated in Invertigo Theatre's High Tide Takeover as one of the writers for *Senses*, a collection of new short plays written, rehearsed and produced in just 10 days. Her play *Touched By Tom Daley* was included in Descent Theatre's *Now We Are Three: The Best of Descent* at the Southwark Playhouse. *Life after Life* received a staged reading as part of the 2013 Vibrant Festival at the Finborough Theatre where she is currently Playwright on Attachment.

Radio includes *Alone in the Garden With You* (BBC Radio 4) and *The Man Inside the Radio is my Dad* (BBC Radio 4).

Catherine Harvey | Playwright

Catherine trained as an actor at the Royal Central School of Speech and Drama after reading English at Oxford.

Writing for the theatre includes *The Rialto Burns*, which was longlisted for the Bruntwood Prize and will have a reading at Bolton Octagon this autumn; *Infinite Riches* (Old Red Lion Theatre), which was longlisted for Little Brother's Big Opportunity; *The Purification Ritual of the*

Sacred Nymphs of Natterjack - Bush Bazaar (Theatre Delicatessen/Bush Theatre); *Angeldust* (Old Red Lion Theatre), which won the Best Writer award at Redfest and was longlisted for the Adrienne Benham Award; *Sweet Dreams*, written for Jo Caulfield (Comedians' Theatre Company, Pleasance Courtyard, Edinburgh), *Crocodile Tears* (Soho Theatre), *The Ash People* (Best Writer, Daffodil Theatre Awards), and short plays at Theatre 503, Menier Chocolate Factory, 24:7 Festival Manchester, *Little Pieces of Gold*, *Writebites* and *The Miniaturists* at the Arcola.

Short film includes *Cuts* (longlisted for Crash Pad, West Yorkshire Playhouse).

Radio/audio includes *Time Flies* (Bolton Octagon/BBC Writersroom North), *Dr Who: Queen of Time, Dr Who: 1001 Nights* (*Smuggling Tales*), *Dr Who: Recorded Time* (all for Big Finish Productions).

Catherine works as an actor in Film, TV, Theatre and Radio, most recently performing at theatres including the National, the Bush, the Finborough, Soho Theatre and the Orange Tree, on TV in the mini-series *Restless* directed by Edward Hall, and on BBC Radio 4's *Poetry Please*. She is an associate artist of London Classic Theatre, and also works as a director of stand-up and sketch comedy.

Louise Hill | Director

Louise was appointed Artistic Director of Attic Theatre Company in 2014.
She trained as a director at Bristol Old Vic Theatre School.
Her previous directing includes *What Every Woman Knows, Quality Street, Outward Bound* and *Pack* (all Finborough Theatre), *The Merchant of Venice* (UK tour), *Boston Marriage* (RWCMD), *Spiders* and *Crocodile Tears* (Soho Theatre Studio), *To a Sunless Sea* (Etcetera Theatre), *Chiming* (Theatre 503), *Face to Face* (Old Red Lion Theatre), *The Merchant of Venice* and *The Taming of the Shrew* (Middle Temple Gardens), *Tiny Dynamite* (Alma Tavern Theatre) and *IAGO*, her own adaptation of *Othello* (Bristol Shakespeare Festival and Edinburgh Fringe Festival, Outstanding Theatre Award winner).
Louise was associate director on Philip Wilson's productions of *Travesties* and *The Importance of Being Earnest* (Birmingham Rep) and assistant director on *Blackbird* and *The Winslow Boy* (Salisbury Playhouse). She was named Best Newcomer Director by the British Theatre Guide and spent two years as artistic director of the Bristol Shakespeare Festival.

Harriet De Winton | Designer

Harriet trained at Bristol Old Vic Theatre School.
She has been resident designer for Shakespeare at the Tobacco Factory for six seasons.

Shows include *As you Like It* (UK Tour), *Arcadia, Richard III, Two Gentlemen of Verona* (UK Tour), *King Lear, The Cherry Orchard, Richard II, The Comedy of Errors, A Midsummer Night's Dream, The Tempest, Julius Caesar, Antony and Cleopatra* and *Uncle Vanya* (co-production with Bristol Old Vic).

Other theatre includes *Fat Man, The Collision of Things* (Little Mighty), *Jigsy* (UK Tour), *The Adventures of Pinocchio* (Tobacco Factory), *Vanity Fair* (Bristol Old Vic Studio), *The Comedy of Errors, The Laramie Project, The House of Bernarda Alba, The Winter's Tale* (The Egg, Theatre Royal Bath), *Match* (UK Tour), *The Canterbury Tales* and *Titus Andronicus* (Nuffield Theatre).

Harriet is Co-Director of theatre company Dot and Ethel. She is also an illustrator and stylist.

Danyal Shafiq | Stage Manager

Danyal trained at Guildhall School of Music & Drama in Stage Management & Technical Theatre.

Previous credits include *April in the Amazon, Cakehead, Clockwork, Precipitation & Will You Fall* (Tete a Tete Opera Festival), *Magic World* (Riverside Studios), *Grumpy Old Women* (UK Tour), *The Grand Budapest Hotel* (Secret Cinema), *Cuckoo* (Unicorn Theatre), *King Lear* (Globe Theatre UK & International Tour), *Privates on Parade* (Noel Coward Theatre), *La Centerentola, Le Nozze di Figaro, Fairy Queen, L'Heure Espagnole/L'Enfant Sortilege* (Glyndebourne Opera House), and *Hansel and Gretel* (Theatre Royal Glasgow – Scottish Opera).

Special thanks to

The Heritage Lottery Fund, Morden Hall Park and the National Trust, the staff of Mitcham Library, Richard Brown and the students and teachers of Cricket Green School, Croydon Salvation Army Band, Christopher Killerby and the Going for a Song singing group, Merton Historical Society, Anthony Hopkins, Dave Saxby, Richard Hewett, David Cottrell, Judith Goodman, Madeline Healey, Sheila Holden, Tony Kane, Ian Crowe, Peter Bird, Paul Howard, Peter Hopkins, Rev. Ray Skinner, Charles Jeffery and all at St Lawrence Church Morden, David Haunton, Melinda Haunton, Iris Brember, Jackie Sullivan and Roedean School, Dr Richard Smith, Professor Edgar Jones, Lianne Smith, The Turnbull Library New Zealand, The Red Cross Archive, Richard Meunier and The London Hospital Archive, Combat Stress the Veteran's Mental Health Charity, The Imperial War Museum, The London Metropolitan Archive, The Royal College of Nursing, The National Archives, the Army Medical Services Museum, Daniel O'Gorman, Nuala and Ian Thomson, Philip Wilson, Audrey King, Sarah Gould, Gemma Hirst, Emma Gillett, Mike, James and Will Monaghan, Tom Murray, Richard Newman, Susie Williamson, Dan Cooke, Joanna McDerra, Yasmin Coonjah, Molly Skelton, Samantha Cheh, May Chee, Rosemary Lever, Bill Dedman

About Attic Theatre Company

Attic was founded by the actors Colin Haigh and Jenny Lee and the musician John Gould, who created a theatre in the ballroom next door to Wimbledon Theatre. In 1994 the ballroom theatre became Wimbledon Studio and Attic Theatre Company was officially formed. Our offices are above Mitcham Library, in the heart of the borough of Merton. We make theatre for a variety of spaces across London and the UK.

Attic has produced over 48 productions, including world premieres and revivals of little-known classics. We make theatre for both traditional and non-traditional theatre spaces. We combine the development of new work with revivals of neglected classics. Merton and our local community are central to our work. Many of Attic's productions are staged within the borough in theatres, parks and historic buildings and Attic also runs an extensive community programme which includes the Ma Kelly plays which tour to day centres and nursing homes, our over 55s singing group Going for a Song, and Many Voices, our drama workshop programme for young refugees.

Attic is run by Artistic Director Louise Hill and General Manager Victoria Hibbs, along with our board of Trustees.

Attic is core-funded by the London Borough of Merton. Project funders include Awards for All, the Cockayne Trust, the Heritage Lottery Fund, The Comic Relief Dispossessed Fund, the Jack Petchey Foundation, the Co-Operative Foundation, Merton Priory Homes and Figges Marsh Community Fund.

The Fields Unsown project has been made possible by the generous support of the Heritage Lottery Fund, Merton Borough Council and the National Trust.

You can learn more about our work on our website, www.attictheatrecompany.com. We are always very happy to hear from individuals and organisations who are interested in our work.

Please contact us at
Mitcham Library
157 London Road
London CR4 2YR

020 8640 6800
info@attictheatrecompany.com

Futility

Move him into the sun -
Gently its touch awoke him once,
At home, whispering of fields unsown.
Always it woke him, even in France,
Until this morning and this snow.
If anything might rouse him now
The kind old sun will know.

Think how it wakes the seeds, -
Woke, once, the clays of a cold star.
Are limbs, so dear-achieved, are sides,
Full-nerved - still warm - too hard to stir?
Was it for this the clay grew tall?
- O what made fatuous sunbeams toil
To break earth's sleep at all?

Wilfred Owen, May 1918

About the Fields Unsown Project

When we first began researching the history of the auxiliary hospital at Morden Hall Park, no one could tell us very much about it. The estate's papers from the period had not survived; the Red Cross knew it had existed and had around 100 beds for soldiers of below officer rank, but it was missing from their lists of auxiliary hospitals; and the London Hospital knew that it had been under their supervision after the war when it became a hospital for women and children, but had no records of its previous existence.

Then we came across an article which had been published on 20 June 1916 in the Feilding Star, a newspaper published far from Morden - in New Zealand - which read:

'Major Chapple's daughters are "doing their little bit": Miss Isa is on the nursing staff of the Second Eastern Hospital at Brighton, Miss Nelca is nursing at the Morden Grange Hospital, and Miss Ella is similarly engaged at the Morden Hall Hospital near Wimbledon.'

We discovered that Ella Chapple's father was William Chapple MP, who had moved his family from Wellington, New Zealand to England shortly before the First World War. Ella and her three sisters were schooled at Roedean in Sussex. When war broke out the three older sisters all worked as VADs, while their father – now MP for Stirlingshire – took up the cause of the Nurses Registration Bill, much to the disapproval of the largely London

Hospital trained matrons of the period. We learned that Morden Hall was supervised by the Bethnal Green Military Hospital, and provided a convalescent home to many soldiers being treated for shellshock by the pioneering Frederick Mott at the Maudsley Hospital.

Through research supported by the Heritage Lottery Fund, and with the generous assistance of archivists, local history experts and academics, as well as the invaluable opportunity to speak to the relatives of some of those who lived and worked at Morden Hall Park during the period, we uncovered some of the lost stories of Morden Hall's unique contribution to the First World War. We discovered George Everard Frankham and James Field – the two gardeners who left the Hall to go to war – William Williams, the Estate Carpenter who was sent to Durban and India, and Colonel Ernest Welch, the soldier who lost his voice after the Battle of Neuve Chapelle and recovered it in a dream after being nursed for 11 months at Morden Hall.

Some of the characters in the play *Fields Unsown* are based on real people whose names and stories we know, and others were inspired by a combination of characters who we know lived and worked at Morden Hall Park before, during and immediately after the First World War. The characters of Ella Chapple and Gilliat Edward Hatfeild are based on real people with those names who we know lived and worked at Morden Hall. Gilliat Edward Hatfeild was the owner of the estate and lived at Morden Hall Park until his death in 1941, when he bequeathed the grounds to the National Trust for the benefit of the local people. Billy and Lizzie Baker are based on some of the children of the estate, whose families (notably the families of William Williams, the Estate Carpenter, and Henry Alderman, the Head Gardener) we have been lucky enough to speak to, and for whose invaluable assistance and generosity we are very grateful. Alex Forbes was inspired by the soldiers from the Commonwealth who were nursed at Bethnal Green Military Hospital, for whom England was only a temporary home, and Robby Stephens by the men whose medical notes we uncovered, who came to Morden Hall for specialist treatment for shellshock and long-term psychological injury under Frederick Mott. Finally, the character of Enid Woods owes much to the professional matrons of the war; her story also echoes that of Emily Power, who served on the Western Front during the First World War and later returned to England to work at Morden Hall Park. Ms Power was matron at Morden Hall Park until her death in 1938.

Later in 2014, our audio trail about Morden Hall Park during the First World War will be available to visitors to the park and online. You can find out more about the research behind the project at our dedicated website funded by the Heritage Lottery Fund, www.fieldsunsown.com.

Playfest 2014

On Saturday 11 and Sunday 12 October 2014, Attic Theatre Company presents **Playfest 2014**, an evening of new short plays presented in association with Wimbledon Bookfest.

Playfest 2014 will be staged in Marlborough Hall, a former performance space which is now the reference section of Wimbledon Library. Join us for a showcase of new and exciting writing, with a chance to discuss the plays with the writers and actors after the performance.

Booking is now open at **www.wimbledonbookfest.org**

Attic Angels

Attic Angels play a vital part in helping us make theatre for our audiences in Merton and beyond. Angels enjoy advance ticket booking, special ticket offers and programme credits and receive invitations to press night parties and other Attic events. We would be very grateful if you would consider becoming an Attic Angel. For further details, please see www.attictheatrecompany.com or telephone Victoria on 020 8640 6800.

Fields Unsown

by Catherine Harvey and Louise Mongahan

For Private Charles E. French of the Gloucestershire Regiment who died 8th September 1916, and Lance Corporal William Frodsham of the Royal Army Medical Corps who died 17th September 1916.

Charlie and Billy were twenty years old when they died at the Battle of the Somme. They are both commemorated on the Thiepval Memorial for soldiers with no known grave.

CHARACTERS

GILLIAT EDWARD HATFEILD, 51 – owner of Morden Hall

BILLY BAKER, 15 – junior gardener at Morden Hall

MATRON ENID WOODS, 39 – a dedicated career nurse in charge of the nurses at Morden Hall

SERGEANT ALEX FORBES, 24 – 3rd British West India Regiment, convalescing for a fractured pelvis

V.A.D. LIZZIE BAKER, 21 – Billy's sister, a nurse

PRIVATE ROBBY STEPHENS, 20 – convalescing for shell shock

V.A.D. ELLA EWING CHAPPLE, 20 – a newly recruited nurse, originally from New Zealand

The play takes place at Morden Hall Park, Surrey, and moves from the present back in time to 1916.

PERFORMANCE NOTES

'Fields Unsown' was written as a site specific play to be performed in Morden Hall Park. The locations used form a circular route around the park and are listed in the stage directions

FIELDS UNSOWN

SCENE 1.

Location: stable yard.

Hatfeild greets the audience individually as his guests, discussing details of the garden with them. In period dress, he carries a silver-topped walking stick. His trousers are held up with string rather than braces, his watch hangs on a bootlace, but he looks otherwise well dressed and respectable. Members of the cast mill about the stable yard disguised as audience members.

(*The following speech may be changed as appropriate for matinee/evening performances.)

Hatfeild stands on a raised platform to give his welcome address.

HATFEILD: (*clears his throat tentatively, directly addressing the audience*) Erm... Hello... Good evening*... Good evening* everyone. Welcome – welcome to Morden Hall Park/...

Members of the cast clap.

HATFEILD: Thank you... that's very... kind... But I really haven't done anything yet!

Members of the cast laugh.

HATFEILD: (*laughs nervously*) Yes... quite... I'm so pleased to have you all here this evening*

1

for our guided tour of the gardens. And
what a lovely evening* we have for it. On
a practical note, the staff will be on hand
throughout in case of emergency —
although we hope it won't come to that...
(*he laughs*) And if you do have any
questions, please don't hesitate to ask, and
I'll do my best to furnish you with
whatever answers are in my power.
Simply wave your hand in the air — like
so... (*he demonstrates*) and...

Billy waves his hand in the air.

HATFEILD: Exactly — like the young gentleman over
there.

Billy continues to wave.

HATFEILD: That's right.

Billy continues to wave.

HATFEILD: Yes..? Did you have a question, son?

BILLY: No, sir — just testing the system.

Members of the cast laugh.

HATFEILD: Quite so — quite so... (*beat*) You can put
your arm down now, Billy — you've proved
the system works.

Members of the cast laugh.

2

HATFEILD: Thank you. (*beat*) So, to the point.
             Morden Hall Park has long been a
             sanctuary from the hustle and bustle of
             daily life. As we go on our tour of the
             grounds this evening* you will note many
             fine examples of flora and fauna. From
             the sturdy English oak to the weeping
             willow, Nature lies in perfect balance here
             – although it's been said I may be a little
             biased. (*he laughs*)

*Members of the cast laugh. Enid, who has binoculars, raises
her hand.*

HATFEILD: (*indicating Enid*) Yes? The lady with the
             binoculars.

ENID: Is there any wildlife here of special
             interest?

HATFEILD: Indeed there is. (*he laughs*) We have many
             native varieties – and rarer birds too – to
             satisfy a keen 'ornithologist' like yourself.
             You never know, if you're lucky some of
             the inhabitants may show themselves this
             evening*.

Alex raises his hand.

HATFEILD: (*nodding towards Alex*) The gentleman over
             there?

ALEX: How long is it since anyone lived in the
             Hall?

3

HATFEILD: Oh, it must be a century now since the family lived here. I speak of the Hatfeild family, of course, who owned Morden Hall until recent times.

Lizzie raises her hand.

HATFEILD: Yes, my dear?

LIZZIE: I thought the late Mr Hatfeild lived in Morden Cottage?

HATFEILD: The late Mr Hatfeild... (*he smiles*) Indeed. I'll show you the Cottage towards the end of our tour. There's a beautiful rose garden there now of which we're all extremely proud. Although the roses were planted after The Great War, of course.

Robby raises his hand.

HATFEILD: Gosh, you are keen, aren't you! (*indicating Robby*) The lad over there...

ROBBY: Wasn't there a hospital here as well?

HATFEILD: You're very well informed.

Members of the cast laugh.

HATFEILD: Some of you may remember Morden Hall as a hospital for sick women and children. And before that, as an auxiliary hospital during the First World War. A sanctuary for our valiant soldiers wounded at the

4

Front. A hundred years ago in fact. (*he laughs sadly*) A hundred years - how time flies… (*he is thoughtful*)

Members of the cast raise their hands.

HATFEILD: (*noticing their raised hands*) Oh — er… right… I think it might be best if I answer the rest of your questions as we head on our tour of the grounds. As a general rule, do keep me always in your sights. Should I feel you've gone astray, I'll wave my walking stick in the air - like so - (*he raises his stick and gives it a wave*) And I must warn you that you'll need to be quick off the mark as you move from place to place as we don't want anyone to be left behind. Actually I've a very funny story about that… (*he laughs*) But I digress… (*he calls*) Billy!

Billy breaks free from the crowd.

BILLY: Yes, Squire.

HATFEILD: Are they all here?

BILLY: All but one, sir - and she won't be a mo.

HATFEILD: Very good. (*direct address to the audience*) Then if you could follow young Billy here — we'll begin…

BILLY: (*banging a drum, directly addresses the audience*) By the left, quick march…

Billy bangs the drum and sings 'It's a Long Way to Tipperary' as he leads the audience, followed by Hatfeild, on a march through the archway at the back of the stable yard into the gardens.

ALL: (*sing*) It's a long way to Tipperary, It's a long way to go (without your mother).
It's a long way to Tipperary And the sweetest girl I know! Farewell Piccadilly, Goodbye, Leicester Square!

It's a long long way to Tipperary, But my heart's right there.

<u>SCENE 2.</u>

Location: café garden.

We see a young woman scurrying across the grass towards us carrying a bag. She trips and stumbles and her hat topples off. Billy stops short.

Ella scoops her hat up and pulls it back on. Billy, meanwhile, looks on in obvious appreciation. He continues to take a keen interest in Ella throughout this scene. Hatfeild watches from the audience.

ELLA: Hello? Hello? Excuse me. Can anyone help me please?

She approaches a member of the audience.

ELLA: I'm looking for Enid Woods. Matron Enid Woods? I'm ever so late. I missed my connection you see.

She addresses another audience member.

ELLA: How was your journey? Did you have any trouble getting here? I couldn't believe it when I heard. An air raid over Mitcham for heavenssakes. It's caused no end of bother. The trains are all in such a frightful muddle.

Billy continues to stare at Ella who seems a little perturbed by his interest and pointedly turns her attention to a young man in the audience.

ELLA: Perhaps you could help me?

She catches sight of Enid, does a double-take, then looks back at the young man.

ELLA: I think that might be her. The Matron I
               mean.

She gives a playful shrug.

ELLA: I'm here to enrol.

She starts to walk purposefully towards Enid.

ELLA: I'm going to be a nurse.

She holds onto her hat as she breaks into a run. She calls back over her shoulder to the audience and, in particular, the young man.

ELLA: A V.A.D.

Billy throws the young man a withering look then addresses the audience.

BILLY: Come on then. Follow me...

Led by Billy, the audience follows Ella across the grass to a gazebo where Enid sits at a table studying some notes.

<u>SCENE 3.</u>

Location: gazebo.

Ella stops at a distance from Enid. She glances at her watch. Enid doesn't look up. Ella adjusts her clothing: straightens her hat, tugs at her coat, draws herself up and hovers.

ENID: Come.

Ella steps a little closer. Enid doesn't look up. Ella glances nervously back at the audience before approaching the table. She smoothes the front of her coat with her hand and waits. Enid gestures, 'sit.' Ella slides into the chair knocking the table. Enid flinches.

ELLA: Sorry.

Enid continues to study Ella's file. Ella waits, her head bowed. Eventually Enid closes her file, removes her glasses and looks up at Ella.

ENID: Chapple.

Enid fixes Ella with a steady gaze.

ELLA: Elizabeth.

ENID: Elizabeth Chapple.

ELLA: But I prefer Ella.

Enid glances back at the file. She sits back in her chair and gazes at Ella.

ENID: Ewing Chapple.

ELLA: It's a family name.

ENID: Your father's name?

ELLA: No. My father's called/...

ENID: I know/...

ELLA: ...William.

ENID: ...who your father is.

ELLA: We each of us... I've three sisters? And the name thing... It's tradition. In my family. To... To take the family name. Nelca? My older sister. Her middle name is Allan.

ENID: Quaint.

ELLA: She's at Morden Grange, which is/...

ENID: Most convenient for you.

ELLA: Yes.

ENID: Assuming you get on. With your sister.

ELLA: I... We. Yes. Yes, we do.

ENID: Allan you say?

ELLA: It's not a Christian name. Well, it is but it's not *her* Christian name, it's a/...

ENID: …Family name.

ELLA: Yes.

ENID: Interesting.

ELLA: It's Scotch.

ENID: Scottish. We say Scottish.

Enid flips the file open again, puts on her glasses and begins to study the notes.

ENID: Are *you* political, Miss Ewing Chapple?

Enid snaps the folder shut and looks at Ella across the top of her glasses. Ella is a little taken aback.

ELLA: I guess we all are. Aren't we? I don't mean to be rude.

ENID: Good.

ELLA: It's just that I think it's everyone's duty… Especially now. To be… Interested. You can't effect change without/…

ENID: Interest.

ELLA: No. Yes. That's… Well, that's my opinion, Nurse.

ENID: Matron.

Beat.

ELLA: (*pointed*) Matron.

Ella fixes Enid with a steady gaze throwing Enid off balance. Ella starts to unbutton her coat.

ELLA: D'you mind?

ENID: Mind what?

ELLA: No, it's just I thought perhaps you'd think me presumptuous. Taking my coat off, I mean.

Enid throws her a withering look.

ELLA: Silly, I know. To think such a thing.

Ella stands up to remove her coat.

ELLA: That's better.

She sits back down and lays the coat across her knee.

ELLA: It is a little oppressive in here.

Enid snatches her glasses off her nose and looks Ella up and down.

ENID: Well. The money wasn't wasted. Clearly.

ELLA: Sorry? Oh, you mean...

Enid looks back at Ella's file.

ENID: Roedean.

Ella gives an uneasy shrug.

ELLA: It's a good school.

ENID:	One of the best. Or so I've been lead to believe.
ELLA:	I was very happy there.
ENID:	Excellent facilities too. I imagine.
ELLA:	Oh, absolutely. Tennis, swimming, cricket...

Ella is suddenly aware of Enid's steely gaze.

ELLA:	Yes. The facilities were... Yes. They were very good.
ENID:	But, of course, if one's father is an M.P....
ELLA:	I'm very proud. Of my father I mean.
ENID:	I'm sure you are. This bill...
ELLA:	The Nurses' Registration Bill? Daddy's so passionate about it.
ENID:	Evidently. And yet, as I'm sure that an educated young woman of your standing will appreciate, the eminent professionals who actually *do* the work are a little less enthusiastic.
ELLA:	I know that some of the matrons in London/...
ENID:	I'm talking, of course, about Miss Nightingale and Miss Luckes.

ELLA: She's dead. Miss Nightingale?

ENID: But her legacy prevails.

ELLA: Evidently. But the world's about to change. Wouldn't you agree?

ENID: And not necessarily for the better.

Pause.

ELLA: It'll be enormously beneficial.

ENID: To whom? Exactly.

ELLA: Our profession.

ENID: *The* profession.

ELLA: It needs to attract intelligent women.

Enid nods sagely.

ELLA: Oh, no. I didn't mean... But it's bound to raise standards. Make us better nurses. I mean three years' training.

ENID: I think you'll find, Miss Chapple, that it's experience that counts.

ELLA: But being registered means everything's properly governed. More standardised.

ENID: I'm not an advocate of standardisation. We deal with human beings, not machines.

ELLA: Well...

Enid cocks her head.

ELLA: No, it's just…

ENID: You think it's a good idea.

ELLA: Yes.

Enid clears her throat. Ella fumbles in her coat pocket.

ENID: To my mind, character is key.

ELLA: Oh, you mean spirit.

ENID: I mean honesty, rectitude, strength and moral fibre. And, in my view at least, it's only once one has worked with someone that one can really evaluate their true worth. Whatever a central governing body might think.

She fixes Ella with a steady gaze.

ELLA: I'm sure you're right. About that anyway.

Ella stares her out.

Enid coughs. Ella pitches forwards as if to help Enid. Enid holds up her hand, dismissing Ella's concern.

ENID: It's nothing.

ELLA: A lot of people have died.

Enid shoots her a glance.

ELLA: Of... Of Diphtheria I mean. I'm sorry, I
            understood you'd been sent home. It was
            Diphtheria..?

ENID: It wasn't confirmed, but in all
            probability...

ELLA: Was it awful? At the Front I mean.

ENID: I'm not inclined to discuss it. Nor would
            you want to hear it. I think you can trust
            me on that.

ELLA: Of course. It would have been very
            different from this though.

ENID: This isn't easy, Miss Chapple. Some of the
            things you see here will be with you for
            life.

Enid starts coughing again. Ella proffers a bag of sweets.

ELLA: Humbug? They taste the same as
            Bullseyes. Peppermint. It's just the shape
            that's different. Some people call them
            bullets but mom always...

Enid cocks her head at Ella.

ELLA: It might help. With the (*beat*) cough.

*Enid shakes her head and reaches for a jug of water. Ella
snatches it up to pour a glass for Enid. A little water slops
onto the file.*

ELLA: Whoops.

Enid freezes. Ella gives a nervous giggle.

ELLA: Good job it's only water.

Ella dabs at the water with a hanky. She offers the glass to Enid. Enid takes the water and has a little sip. She shakes out her own hanky with a flourish and wipes the file. She drops the sodden hanky back on the desk then puts out her hand. Ella places a sweet in her hand. Enid keeps her hand open.

ENID: The bag.

ELLA: Oh!

ENID: Confectionary is prohibited.

Enid drops the sweets into a bin beside her desk.

ENID: Well. I've no doubt you're eager to see your quarters.

ELLA: My...

ENID: Accommodation.

ELLA: Oh. Yes. Of course.

Ella gets to her feet.

ENID: Billy will show you.

ELLA: Billy?

ENID: (*loudly so Billy can hear*) He's hanging
                 around eavesdropping like as not. Skinny
                 young strip of a lad. You'll find him.

*Billy scrabbles away from the door. Ella exits and makes her
way towards the house.*

ENID: (*direct address*) Well, don't just stand there
                 gawping at me. You must have something
                 useful to do. Don't you know there's a war
                 on?

SCENE 4.

Location: gazebo travelling to the lawn.

Hatfeild and Billy lead Ella and the audience onto the path.

BILLY: (*to Ella*) Come on then, slow coach. Get a
                 move on!

HATFEILD: Billy..!

BILLY: (*innocently*) What?

HATFEILD: (*amused*) Manners, please.

BILLY: May I help you with your bag, miss?

ELLA: No, thank you. I'm fine. (*she marches off
                 ahead*)

BILLY: (*direct address*) One of them new-fangled
                 ladies, eh! I like that in a girl. (*seeing Ella
                 has gone, he calls after her*) Hey, Ella! Wait
                 up! (*he tears off to catch up*)

The audience continue along the path up to the lawn led by Hatfeild.

HATFEILD: Right – to the business in hand. (*direct address as he walks*) If you could move up now towards the river... Thank you... Then to your left if you would – where there's a particularly fine avenue of lime and chestnut trees I'd like to bring to your attention... The river to your right is the Wandle, which flows from the North Downs to the Thames... While to your left is Morden Hall itself – the large white building you can see through the trees...

<u>SCENE 5.</u>

Location: lawn in front of Morden Hall.

Alex and Robby sit knitting socks. They wave to Hatfeild as he approaches.

ALEX: (*calls*) Afternoon, sir/…

ROBBY: (*calls*) All right, Squire!

HATFEILD: No, don't stand up - unless it's part of your regime. I don't want to upset Matron again. (*he laughs*) How's the knitting going?

ROBBY: Alex 'ere's nearly done a sweater – cable stitch – the lot.

HATFEILD: You're getting to be quite the expert.

ALEX: Ah, I don't know about that.

HATFEILD: Well, you'll be glad of the new clobber when winter comes.

20

They laugh. Alex and Robby continue to knit.

ALEX: I see the apples lookin' fit.

HATFEILD: They do now, yes - thanks to your efforts.

ROBBY: The branches are bendin' right over. If I were a kid I'd be up them like a shot.

HATFEILD: Well, I'm sure you chaps'll make light work of them in a pie for Sunday tea.

They laugh.

ALEX: You headin' off a' the river, now – to deal with that 'little problem' ya had yesterday?

HATFEILD: What? Oh, yes – the rats. They were eating breakfast again this morning outside the front door - bold as you like – when I got up. (*he laughs*)

ROBBY: Rats..? (*he looks around anxiously*)

HATFEILD: But that's the price of living so close to the water, I'm afraid.

ROBBY: (*mumbling*) You wanna be careful…

HATFEILD: What's that, old chap?

ROBBY: You wanna be careful. They'll eat the face off you if you don't keep a look out.

HATFEILD: Don't worry, son, you're safe enough here.

ROBBY: You'll kill them for me, won't you, gov'nor?

ALEX: Am sure he will.

ROBBY: George/…?

ALEX: No, fren' is me.

ROBBY: (*gripping him*) Is that you George?

ALEX: Steady there/steady…

ROBBY: You'll need to get your head down – or the snipers'll pick us off like rabbits.

HATFEILD: Don't worry, son, there's no snipers here…

ROBBY: I thought I heard the guns.

HATFEILD: You're safe now. You're at Morden Hall.

ALEX: Everythin' cook and curry.

ROBBY: Alex?

ALEX: That's right, old pal.

ROBBY: We're in the hospital together, aren't we mate?

ALEX: Yeah, mon.

HATFEILD: Good lad.

Beat.

HATFEILD: Well, mustn't shilly shally.   Sooner I'm
              off, sooner they'll be gone.

*Hatfeild waves a hand and heads off.   Alex and Robby watch
him go.*

ALEX: That gentleman is a very good gardener...
              (*he nods wisely*)

*Alex knits.   Robby does his breathing exercises, perhaps
occasionally humming 'It's a Long Way to Tipperary' to calm
himself.   Hatfeild lingers at the back of the audience to watch
the scene.*

ALEX: You want me to do them exercises with
              you?

ROBBY: I'll be fine, ta.   Nurse Baker's been
              through 'em with me.

ALEX: Ah, has she now?

ROBBY: Yeah.

Alex continues knitting.   Robby does his breathing exercises.

ALEX: You read the papers this mornin'?

ROBBY: I've not.   No.

ALEX: Terrible things.

*Alex tuts wisely.   They continue knitting.   Robby shifts
uncomfortably, winces, settles himself.*

ROBBY: I heard it's gettin' – is it? – rougher - out there. On the Somme, I mean...

ALEX: (*nods wisely*) Ah, yeah...

ROBBY: It's a rum do.

ALEX: It is, my fren'.

They continue kitting.

ALEX: You more comfortable now, mon?

ROBBY: Much better, thanks.

ALEX: You'll be having a bath soon no doubt?

ROBBY: Why, do I smell or summat?

They laugh.

ALEX: You have so many baths I think they will wash you away.

ROBBY: Part of me regime, in't it. They're meant to relax me.

ALEX: And does it work?

ROBBY: Nah. I just get more tense havin' to take me clothes off in front of the nurses. You know, with the shrapnel and that.

ALEX: Ah, it muss be hell – what with the cups a' warm milk they bring ya in the evening and the pretty nurses massagin' your

24

shoulders all the time. (*he laughs knowingly*)

ROBBY: I know, mate – but I suffer it – stay brave, stay strong. Flyin' the flag for British manhood in the face of adversity – that's me.

They laugh.

ALEX: And the other thing – the electricity – you not had that again?

ROBBY: No, not here, thank God.

ALEX: The men scream, I am told – even with no voice they open their mouth to scream.

ROBBY: But old man Mott, he does things more lightly. He's a sense of humour, Dr Mott.

ALEX: Yeah?

ROBBY: Like there was this one fella in't bed next to me up the Maudsley who wouldn't speak for love nor money. So Dr Mott, he stands right beside 'is bed and whispers to the nurse – loud enough the whole ward could hear, mind – (*imitating the consultant*) 'When that young man can ask loud enough, he can have a bottle of stout and a mutton chop.'

ALEX: And did he?

ROBBY: Too right — he were speakin' clear as any sergeant on parade before the end of t'day.

They laugh and continue knitting.

ALEX: She a lovely girl that.

ROBBY: Who?

ALEX: Dis Nurse Baker ya. A very adaptable dame, as they say.

ROBBY: (*laughing*) Yeah, she is...

ALEX: (*teasing*) 'Yeah'?

ROBBY: Yeah. I grant you Lizzie is a beautiful girl.

ALEX: Ya 'Lizzie' is it?

ROBBY: You see, mate, this is why I don't/ - mate... come on...

ALEX: Lizzie, I love you with all me heart/...

ROBBY: (*laughing*) All right/...

Lizzie approaches carrying a glass of water and some tablets. Alex and Robby don't see her.

ALEX: Lizzie, you the most beautiful girl in the whole of the world. Oh, Lizzie! (*sees Lizzie*) Oh... Lizzie!

LIZZIE: I didn't know you cared, Sergeant Forbes.

ALEX: I don't... I mean... (*embarrassed*) Ah,
               nah...

LIZZIE: (*to Robby*) Looks like someone's got a dose
               of his own medicine.

Robby and Lizzie laugh. Alex knits sheepishly.

LIZZIE: Come along then, Private Stephens – time
               for your tablets. (*to Alex, teasing*) I think
               you've slipped a stitch there, Sergeant.

Robby sits up, winces.

LIZZIE: You feelin' all right?

ROBBY: Fine thanks, miss.

Alex tuts knowingly.

LIZZIE: What? What is it?

ALEX: Tell the lady.

ROBBY: They're just not agreein' with me is all, the
               tablets.

LIZZIE: Stomach again?

ROBBY: And me mouth's worse.

LIZZIE: Let me see.

ROBBY: It's all sore and swollen like.

*Lizzie leans closer to examine him. Robby enjoys the
proximity.*

LIZZIE: Open wide.

Robby opens his mouth shakily.

LIZZIE: Very good. Now - hold out your hands.

Robby holds out his hands – they are shaking.

LIZZIE: That's fine - thank you. (*she takes his hands and puts them down gently*)

Enid approaches.

ENID: Are you feeling unwell, Private Stephens?

LIZZIE: It's under control, Matron.

ROBBY: Can you hear somethin'?

LIZZIE: No... Private... it's all quiet in the trenches tonight.

ENID: I thought I made it clear that your role is to divert their minds from introspection, not indulge them.

LIZZIE: But/...

ENID: Has Private Stephens had his medication today?

LIZZIE: I'm not sure it's agreeing with him.

ENID: Nonsense.

Beat – Lizzie is unsure whether to go or stay.

ENID:	I'll deal with this while you take Sergeant Forbes off for his evening* walk. Go on - chop chop! (*she takes a bottle of pills from her pocket*)
LIZZIE:	Yeah, but them pills?
ENID:	Do as you're told, nurse.

Lizzie reluctantly takes Alex for a walk leaving Enid to administer Robby's medicine. Enid takes Robby's obs during the following scene.

SCENE 6.

Location: lawn beside the white bridge.

Meanwhile Ella and Billy are making their way back from the Dairy. Ella is struggling to carry two small churns of milk. Billy is wheeling a wheel barrow piled high with grass cuttings. Hatfeild leads the audience closer to them to watch the scene, amused as it unfolds.

BILLY:	Wouldn't be no bother.
ELLA:	I can manage perfectly well thank you.

She turns her ankle and stumbles. Billy chuckles. She glares at him.

BILLY: Go on. I'd run 'em over in half the time.

Ella dumps the churns and stops for a moment. She wipes her brow with the back of her hand. Billy makes as if to pick up one of the churns.

ELLA: Leave it!

Ella picks up the churns and continues to struggle across the grass.

BILLY: Didn't ought be doin' stuff like that. Look at those hands. Lady's hands those are.

Ella dumps the churns on the grass narrowly missing Billy's toe. A little milk slops onto the grass.

ELLA: I'm more than capable of hard physical labour. In all probability, I'm a lot stronger than you are.

She draws herself up and tackles the churns again. Billy, meanwhile, pushes his wheel barrow beside

Ella, stealing a glance at her every now and then.

BILLY: There's rats by the Wandle.

ELLA: Rats?

BILLY: Big blighters. Size of a small dog some of 'em.

ELLA: What?

BILLY: You scared?

ELLA: No.

She glances around nervously.

BILLY: Me neither. I'm not scared. Set him off
               though, don't they?

ELLA: Who?

Billy gives a nod in Robby's direction.

BILLY: Geezer what does all the... (*he shakes and
               grimaces*) You know. Stuff.

ELLA: Private Stephens.

BILLY: Bit bonkers, is he?

ELLA: No, he's not. He's traumatised. These
               men have been to hell and back.

BILLY: Just asking.

ELLA: Poor man. He's brought the battlefield
               home.

BILLY: Eh?

ELLA: Memories. Rats remind him.

BILLY: They tell you their stories, do they? All
               stuff what they've seen at the Front.

Pause. Ella isn't sure if she should divulge what she's heard to someone as young as Billy.

ELLA: The older men tend not to. I think they want to protect us.

BILLY: What, treat you like a daughter you mean?

ELLA: They know we're very young. But then they... Well, they have nightmares. Some of them. Talk in their sleep.

BILLY: Cry out for their mother? It's only what I've heard.

ELLA: It's true.

Billy sniggers. Ella glares at him.

BILLY: No, I weren't laughing at them though.

ELLA: Go away, Billy. Why don't you run and play?

Billy exits as Ella continues to lug the milk across the grass.

<u>SCENE 7.</u>

Location: crossing the white bridge, travelling to the lawn in front to the Rose Garden.

Hatfeild steps forward.

HATFEILD: Er... Right... Well, I think we'd better head across the bridge – where you'll see ahead of you that very fine avenue of lime and horse chestnut trees I promised/ earlier...

Billy hurtles towards the audience.

BILLY: (*direct address, shouting*) Roll up, roll up -
                fight for King and Country.   Men over
                that side, ladies over here. (*he winks at a
                girl in the audience*) All right, love. We'll be
                passin' among you, sortin' out the men
                from the boys. Lettin' you know who's fit
                for service and who's not – (*he calls*) isn't
                that right, Lizzie?

Lizzie joins him to lead them in the recruitment game.

LIZZIE: (*calls*) It is, Billy. You ladies, I'm afraid,
                aren't suitable to bear arms – but I'm sure
                we can find some other work for you at the
                Hospital – washin' bed linen, or pickin'
                veggies from the garden. So don't you
                worry, you'll be part of the War Effort all
                the same, helpin' our brave troops who've
                fought out at the Front.

*Lizzie and Billy give the men ranks, lining them up in order
from greatest to least.*

LIZZIE: You look like a Major, you do.

BILLY: That's important. You'd go in first in a
                ruck.

LIZZIE: Private for you – (*moves 'the recruit' to the
                back*) but you'll soon work your way up.

BILLY: My brother Jack was a Private - but he
                won a medal for valour so now he's a
                Lance   Corporal.   He's   fightin'   the

Germans, givin' 'em what for. I'm gonna join the Army soon and be a soldier like him.

LIZZIE: 'Ere – you look like our Jack – you can be a Lance Corporal.

BILLY: Lizzie's dead proud of Jack.

LIZZIE: He makes me so full of pride I could burst.

BILLY: I'm afraid the gentleman with the beard/glasses (*as appropriate*), you're too old to fight – over to that side if you would...

LIZZIE: If you'd be so kind as to step over there please, miss – and you too, missus, if you would. That's right – form an orderly line...

BILLY: (*lining the men up in order of rank, he speaks to each in turn*) Private... Private... Sergeant... Ooh, that's a nice coat - Sergeant Major you. Sir! (*he salutes*)

LIZZIE: (*direct address to another*) Are you religious at all? Army Chaplain, I think.

BILLY: I'll make you proud one day, Lizzie. I'll make you proud like our Jack when I go off and fight old Fritz.

LIZZIE: Don't be daft. It'll all be over by the time
               you're big enough to join up.

BILLY: (*grunts and shrugs her off*) Now - those of
               you unfit for service – the ladies and those
               as is clapped out, so to speak – will be led
               by my boss 'ere – no offence, sir.

HATFEILD: None taken, son.

*Billy leads the men and boys of fighting age. Lizzie leads the
women and children. Hatfeild leads the older men and others
who are unfit for service. They march over the bridge whistling
'It's a Long Way to Tipperary' or another famous wartime
song. Lizzie and Billy speak over the whistling.*   .

BILLY: (*winks at a girl*) Girls like you when you're
               a soldier. Jack writes to a girl. I saw him
               kiss her the day he left – down by the river
               where the grass is high. I don't think I'd
               like to kiss a girl. I think it would be nicer
               to eat a Humbug. But flirtin's all right,
               isn't it.

LIZZIE: (*laughing*) Husht, Billy!

BILLY: (*whispers loudly to another*) What is flirtin'?
               Is it buying a girl a gift? I won't be able to
               flirt properly 'til I'm a soldier because I
               don't have enough money at present. I'm
               only a junior gardener, see. But when I'm
               in the Army I'm gonna be a Lance
               Corporal like my brother Jack, then I shall

save up all my pay and be a jolly good flirt.

LIZZIE: Enough!

Ella is winding bandages on the lawn. She waves to Lizzie.

ELLA: (*calls*) Hey, Lizzie! Lizzie!

BILLY: (*seeing Ella, winks knowingly at the audience*) Aye, aye... (*he bolts off up the path*)

ELLA: (*calls*) Can you help me with these, please?

LIZZIE: (*calls*) Yeah, 'course... (*direct address to audience*) Come on then – chop, chop...

Lizzie leads the audience to where Ella winds the bandages. Hatfeild drops behind.

<u>SCENE 8.</u>

Location: lawn in front of the Rose Garden.

Lizzie approaches Ella.

LIZZIE: Give us some then.

ELLA: You're a life saver, thanks.

LIZZIE: Lummy days! There's loads of 'em. Must've gone berserk in the Workroom today.

They laugh.

LIZZIE: (*direct address*) 'Ere you better do one an' all... (*hands someone a bandage to wind*)

Ella and Lizzie wind clean bandages. Occasionally they ask an audience member to hold a completed roll, or invite them to wind a length of bandage.

ELLA: That Sister Woods is a bit of a dragon, isn't she.

LIZZIE: She's not so bad when you get to know her. Fastidious is all. Likes the job done proper. (*holding out the end of a bandage to an audience member*) 'Ere – do this one would you? Wind 'em round – tight, mind – that's it. Ta.

ELLA: I don't know if I'll ever get used to her 'ways'. (*she gives a theatrical shudder*)

They laugh.

LIZZIE: The first few weeks are the worst. She softens after that.

ELLA: Really?

LIZZIE: What d'you think.

Lizzie gives Ella a direct look. They laugh. Lizzie hands a bandage roll to an audience member.

LIZZIE: Could you put this in the basket for me? Ta.

ELLA: But you enjoy it here, don't you?

LIZZIE: It's less hard work than looking after me brothers and sisters for me mum. (*to an audience member*) Don't drop it now whatever you do or Matron'll give you what for.

ELLA: It's not – I dunno..?

LIZZIE: Gruesome?

ELLA: I suppose. (*beat*) They showed me the book.

LIZZIE: The Chamber of Horrors.

ELLA: Those photographs... Some of them hardly look like men at all. (*beat*) You've got a brother at the Front haven't you?

LIZZIE: Jack. Next eldest after me.

ELLA: You must worry.

LIZZIE: I wonder every day what he's up to. But I
                know if he got hurt there'd be some nurse
                like me to take care of him.

*They wind the bandages, handing each completed roll to an
audience member to put in the basket.*

LIZZIE: I love your frock.

ELLA: Which one?

LIZZIE: The one you was wearing when you
arrived.

ELLA: Oh, that.   Mom had it sent from the
                States.   I was trying a bit too hard to
                impress. I think Matron may have taken
                against me for it. 'Poor little rich girl' -
                you know.

LIZZIE: She's American is she, your mum?

ELLA: Yes.

LIZZIE: But you're from Australia?

ELLA: New Zealand.

LIZZIE: Blimey!

ELLA: I went to high school over here though, so
                it's not as glamorous as it sounds

LIZZIE: I bet it's not. (*she laughs*)

ELLA: You can borrow it if you like — the frock —
             when you go out with your chap.

LIZZIE: Oh, I don't have a chap.

ELLA: Don't you want to bag yourself a
             handsome soldier?

LIZZIE: Dunno. When I come here I thought I'd
             find romance — but it's all been a bit real
             since. It's like Matron says, you have to
             be a good friend to the men but never cross
             the line. 'Cos it's a trust they've put in you
             — themselves at their weakest moments.

ELLA: You like her, don't you — that old dragon.

LIZZIE: I admire her — I'm not sure it's the same
             thing. She's given her life to it, you know.
             And it must be hard to be alone when
             you're so old.

ELLA: How old is she, d'you reckon?

LIZZIE: Forty, I heard. It's her birthday today.
             The girls in the Workroom were gossiping.

ELLA: That's harsh.

LIZZIE: I was thinking we could do something
             since she's on her own. I'm baking a cake
             to celebrate — gonna put jam in it and
             cream from the Dairy.

ELLA: I'm not sure she'll want to celebrate being forty.

LIZZIE: I thought we could light candles and all sing 'Happy Birthday'.

ELLA: She doesn't look the partying type.

Billy approaches. He is carrying a bag of apples.

BILLY: All right there, Miss Ella?

LIZZIE: (*ignoring him*) Come on - where's your sense of fun?

BILLY: There you go look.

He dumps the bag of apples on top of the pile of bandages.

BILLY: Apples.

Ella takes the bag off the pile of bandages and dumps them on the ground.

BILLY: Mind out. Don't want 'em bruising.

Lizzie reaches for an apple.

LIZZIE: Lovely, Bill. Thanks.

Billy slaps her hand away.

BILLY: They're for her.

LIZZIE: Ella?

ELLA: (*under her breath*) Oh, for heavenssakes!

BILLY: Windfalls.

ELLA: In which case…

Ella picks up an apple.

ELLA: They'd be bruised already.

Ella inspects the apple. She throws Billy a pointed look.

BILLY: Small tree, innit? They don't have far to
                fall.

Ella tosses the apples back into the bag.

BILLY: Well, if you don't want 'em…

He picks up the bag of apples.

ELLA: I didn't say that.

He beams.

ELLA: We can't afford to waste them.

*Billy takes an apple and polishes it on his sleeve. He proffers
it to Ella.*

BILLY: Go on then. Take a bite.

ELLA: I will not.

*Ella recoils. Billy takes a bite. Ella bats the apple away but
makes a grab for the bag. Billy snatches the bag out of reach.
A little tussle ensues. Billy enjoys every minute.*

43

LIZZIE: Silly beggar. Give her the apples for
                 heavenssakes. You brung 'em for her you
                 said.

Ella lets go of the bag. They eyeball one another for a moment.
Suddenly aware of the intensity of Billy's gaze, Ella looks
away. Billy holds out the bag of apples. Ella takes them
grudgingly.

ELLA: Thank you. We can give them to the men.

BILLY: Full of... What's the word?

ELLA: Vitamins?

Billy smiles and munches the apple.

BILLY: Sunshine.

In spite of herself, a glimmer of a smile crosses Ella's face.
Billy gives a little nod of appreciation. Lizzie rolls her eyes.
Ella inspects the fruit.

ELLA: Bit wormy.

BILLY: Yeah, but if you cut the bad bits out,
                 right? You could stick 'em in a pie.
                 P'raps? (*beat*) I dunno, do I?

LIZZIE: Good idea, Bill. Why not, eh?

ELLA: Don't look at me.

BILLY: Didn't your mum learn you how?

ELLA: I'm perfectly capable. I just don't see why
               I should.

BILLY: Oooh, Miss Hoity Toity.

ELLA: It's got nothing to do with that.

LIZZIE: Love baking me.

ELLA: Oh, stop it.

Ella flumps down and toys with the bandages.

LIZZIE: What's up with you?

ELLA: I'm just a little frustrated, that's all.

LIZZIE: How come?

ELLA: It's just… I don't think we should make
               all these distinctions. Putting people in
               boxes. Men do this, women do that.

BILLY: So, what? Send the women off to fight
               and let the men have the kids, shall we?

LIZZIE: Don't talk soft. Can't wait to be wife and
               mum some day.

ELLA: A man's the last thing I want. And as for
               having children…

LIZZIE: What you got in mind then?

ELLA: I want to travel. See the world.

BILLY: I'm gonna do that.   Travel the world.
              Well, France any rate.

Lizzie throws him a look.

BILLY: I might.

Lizzie shakes her head.   It's a dismissive gesture.

BILLY: She tell you?

ELLA: No.

LIZZIE: What?

BILLY: Gonna sign up.

LIZZIE: Huh. That.

BILLY: Follow in me brother's footsteps. I wanna
              be a soldier. What d'you think to that?

ELLA: I think you're a perfect fool.

LIZZIE: Yeah, I'd second that. Well, look at ya?

BILLY: What?

LIZZIE: You're far too young to join up.

ELLA: You're not much more than a child.

BILLY: I'm fifteen!

ELLA: Exactly.

LIZZIE: He's dead proud of his brother. I am an'
              all.

ELLA: Jack?

LIZZIE: Good bit older 'un Billy.

ELLA: How old?

BILLY: Seventeen.

LIZZIE: Writes ever so reg'lar. All what's going on.
               What he's seen. Grub's all right, he said.
               And plenty of it. Should be due another
               letter pretty soon. I imagine.

*Ella catches her eye and smiles. Lizzie smiles back. They
continue to roll bandages for a moment.*

LIZZIE: The cake! Lummy days!

Lizzie throws the bandages down.

ELLA: How long's it been in?

LIZZIE: Too long. It'll be burnt to a crisp.

Lizzie leaves.

BILLY: (*he laughs*) Serves her right the old dragon.

Ella picks up a pile of bandages.

ELLA: You can make yourself useful. Take this
               lot back to the Dispensary.

BILLY: Bandages?

ELLA: In one. Off you go.

Billy snatches up the bandages and leaves.

<u>SCENE 9.</u>

Location: lawn travelling to the gates of the Rose Garden.

Billy runs, laden with bandages. In his haste he drops some, picks them up – then gets audience members to pick them up - dropping them all the while. He doesn't notice Enid watching him.

BILLY: (*direct address*) 'Ere, can one of you help me, please…? (*collecting the bandages from the audience*) Thanks… Thanks… Cheers mate – you're a diamond. Our Lizzie'll give me what for if I don't get this done in time. Why she wants to give that old dragon a treat is beyond me. But that's our Lizzie all over – she's got a big heart she has.

<u>SCENE 10.</u>

Location: inside the gates of the Rose Garden.

Enid arrives behind him, unseen by Billy.

ENID: What are you doing?

Shocked, Billy drops the bandages then scrabbles to pick them up.

BILLY: Nothing... I... Oh, it's you Matron. (*he picks up the bandages helped by the audience*) Thanks mate – cheers... (*beat*) Well, I'd better be on me way, miss...

ENID: One moment young man. What are you doing with those bandages?

BILLY: I'd rather not say if it's all the same to you.

ENID: And why not?

BILLY: It's something you'd best not know about... (*he winks knowingly*)

ENID: Did you take them from the Workroom?

49

BILLY: Hang on a minute/...

ENID: You're up to no good - it's written/all over
                your face.

BILLY: All right, all right, there's no need/to get
                arsy...

ENID: They won't be sterile any more.   I beg
                your/ pardon?

BILLY: I was only tryin' to help.

ENID: Did you steal these bandages?

BILLY: (*throws the bandages at Enid*) Oh, have
                your rotten bandages, you wrinkled old
                bag.

*Whispering, laughter, hushed tones from the nearby
rhododendron bushes as the bandages fall like streamers
around Enid – 'Now?' 'Yes, now.' 'Go on!' 'Go on!' Lizzie,
Ella, Robby, Alex pop out of the bushes. Lizzie holds a cake –
the candles are lit.*

ALL: Surprise!

ENID: What's this..?

ALEX/ROBBY: Happy birthday, Sister!

LIZZIE/ELLA: Happy birthday!

BILLY: (*shouts over the celebrations*) I hope you
                choke on it! (*he runs away*)

All sing 'Happy Birthday' while Enid tries to hide her discomfort. Everyone cheers.

Beat.

LIZZIE: It's a Victoria sponge, Matron.

ELLA: We all chipped in.

ENID: It's very... Unexpected. Thank you.

ALEX: The fellas wanted to show our appreciation.

ENID: It's lovely. A lovely thought. Very kind.

LIZZIE: We heard it was a big birthday, so we wanted to do something special.

ELLA: Lizzie baked the cake.

ENID: Very pretty. (*beat*) This must have taken you a long time to organise.

LIZZIE: I didn't mind, we all think you're/...

ENID: Time that should have been devoted to the patients.

LIZZIE: No one was neglected. They were all happy to/help...

ENID: Well, since you've obviously got too much time on your hands, I suggest you take Private Stephens somewhere quiet and give him his medication.

LIZZIE: Oh, but the medication's/not agreeing...

ENID: Off you go then.

Beat. Lizzie takes Robby's arm and makes as if to lead him away. Ella glances at Lizzie then glares at Enid.

ENID: Was there something you wished to say, Nurse Chapple?

ELLA: No. (*pointed*) No, thank you, Matron.

ENID: Very well.

Enid turns on her heel.

ELLA: Yes actually. I do.

Enid turns back.

LIZZIE: Ella.

Lizzie puts her hand on Ella's arm as if in an effort to restrain her. Ella shrugs her off.

ELLA: She needs to be told and if you aren't going to stick up for yourself then I will.

LIZZIE: Don't need stickin' up for. (*to Robby*) C'mon then, you.

Lizzie leads Robby away.

ELLA: Lizzie went to a lot of trouble baking that cake.

ENID: Time that might've been better spent
             doing the job she's paid for.

ELLA: You're absolutely right.

Enid gives a little nod, smug.

ELLA: Because it sure as heck was wasted on you.
             She's worth ten of you. All the men think
             so. For the first time in ages they felt part
             of something good. Something cosy and
             safe/...

ENID: We have plenty of diversions for the men.

ELLA: They need a sense of purpose and
             belonging. That's what Lizzie gave them.
             And you. You ruined it.

ENID: Nurse Chapple...

ELLA: You ruined it.

In spite of herself, Ella is fighting tears.

ENID: Well. Perhaps once you've managed to
             compose yourself, you'd like to share the
             cake amongst the men. Their need is far
             greater than mine.

*Ella takes the cake. Enid stalks off. Ella begins to distribute
the cake. Alex appears. He notices Ella's distress and
approaches.*

ALEX: Can I help you, ma'am?

ELLA: Nurse.

ALEX: Can I help you?

ELLA: Yes. Yes, please.

Alex helps Ella distribute the cake amongst the audience.

<u>SCENE 11.</u>

Location: Rose Garden, beside a stream (the audience watch from the opposite bank).

Lizzie helps Robby to sit on a bench. He is breathless – his stomach sore, his mouth swollen.   She offers him a piece of cake.

ROBBY: No cake for me, ta.

LIZZIE: Is it still bad?

Robby nods. Lizzie examines his swollen face and abdomen.

ROBBY: I'm sorry to be a trouble to you, Nurse.

LIZZIE: Call me Lizzie.

ROBBY: Won't your boss lady give you what for?

LIZZIE: Oh, pot on her!

Robby laughs.

LIZZIE: Are you laughing at me, Robby Stephens?

ROBBY: I wouldn't dream of it, Nurse Baker.

LIZZIE: Lizzie.

ROBBY: Lizzie.

LIZZIE: It's good to see you smile. Lights up your whole face. (*she touches his face*) Now, let's get these tablets sorted...

Lizzie counts out the tablets. Robby puts his hand to his face.

ROBBY: I often wonder... If a girl'll ever be able to – you know –

LIZZIE: (*distracted*) What's that..?

ROBBY: Look at me again - with affection I mean.

LIZZIE: Of course they will. You're a great catch.

ROBBY: (*laughs shyly*) Maybe once.

LIZZIE: (*taking out the tablets*) I'd rather you didn't take these if they're making you ill.

ROBBY: I'm distracting you from your job.

LIZZIE: Not at all – it's always nice to chat to you.

ROBBY: (*he holds out his hand for the tablets*) Matron's orders.

LIZZIE: (*hands him the tablets*) Oh - I've no water!

ROBBY: I'll manage/ (*he tips his head back shakily and swallows the tablets effort*)

LIZZIE: You shouldn't/... Robby!

ROBBY: Gone – see – (*he sticks out his tongue proudly*)

LIZZIE: (*laughs*) You're a rascal, you know that.

ROBBY: (*laughs shyly*) It's been said.

Robby looks at his hands – they are shaking.

ROBBY: I'm not a malingerer.

LIZZIE: I know you're not.

ROBBY: One day I'll own me own house. There's no one alive's more conscientious than me.

LIZZIE: You can do anything if you put your mind to it. You're that sort of a fella.

ROBBY: Yeah, I am.

Robby shakes, nervous. Lizzie smiles encouragingly.

ROBBY: So you think... Nurse/ –

LIZZIE: Lizzie.

ROBBY: You think a nice girl – could find me – you know/..?

LIZZIE: Handsome?

ROBBY: Normal, I was gonna say. Let's not push
                the boat out before we can... I mean/ -

LIZZIE: I know what you mean.

*They laugh. Robby's hands are shaking. Lizzie puts her
hands on his to steady them. Mistaking the gesture, Robby
leans in to kiss her.*

LIZZIE: No!

ROBBY: I'm sorry/I'm an...

LIZZIE: I'm your nurse/ –

ROBBY: Idiot/ –

LIZZIE: No – no, you're not. It's natural for you
                to feel – attached to me.

ROBBY: Nothing will ever be normal again.

LIZZIE: I'm sure it will. (*beat*) If a girl like me can
                be a nurse for a job, you can build a new
                life for yourself - have a nice girl and a nice
                home. It's like the Doctor always says -
                (*imitating Mott*) 'Keep looking forward,
                don't dwell on the past.'

Beat.

ROBBY: You should be getting on. I don't want to
                keep you.

LIZZIE: We're still mates, aren't we?

57

Robby shrugs. Lizzie goes to take his hand, but Robby pulls away.

ROBBY: My pal George – he was my best pal. I see him everywhere though he's not around no more.

LIZZIE: Is he the fella – the one you call out for?

ROBBY: Yeah. Silly sod lit a fire to make a cup of tea right on top of an unexploded bomb. (*beat*) We did everything together him and me – from t'first day of school. 'The terrible twosome' they called us – we were known all over. Always in some bother or t'other, getting into mischief, taking a beating for our trouble from the teachers an' that. Joined up together too – him and me. Our mums waved us off together. Inseparable we were. 'Til the explosion – then it were just him what took the beating. (*he turns his head sharply, hearing a sound*) What's that?

LIZZIE: What?

ROBBY: A rat – look – there in the water! (*he peers at the water*) What you eating, boy..?

LIZZIE: Come on now… I think you need a rest… (*she tries to lift Robby but he resists*)

ROBBY: I don't like the dark, miss. Don't put me in the dark.

58

LIZZIE: Let's get you/up…

ROBBY: Are you an angel?

LIZZIE: No one's ever called me that before.

ROBBY: (*clings to her, increasingly breathless, losing
              consciousness*) Who's there?

LIZZIE: It's me, Lizzie…

ROBBY: I can't see your face.

LIZZIE: Robby? (*beat*) Can you hear me, Robby?

ROBBY: (*he retches*) Oh, God…

*Robby runs to the river to be sick then passes out. Lizzie runs
over to help him.*

LIZZIE: Robby!

*Lizzie hurriedly examines Robby then calls for help with
increasing desperation.*

LIZZIE: Help! Can someone help me here? There's
              a patient in distress! Help me someone –
              please!

*Ella comes running, followed by Enid. Robby lies on the
ground, groaning.*

ROBBY: (*mumbles*) George…

LIZZIE: Can you hear me, Robby? It's all right…

Ella enters and immediately goes to help Lizzie. Enid enters shortly afterwards and stops to catch her breath, watching Ella and Lizzie tend Robby who is breathing with some difficulty.

LIZZIE: I think he's having a reaction to his medication.

ELLA: Private Stephens, can you hear me?

LIZZIE: Robby! Robby!

ENID: (*regaining her composure*) We're going to have to open his airway. If you could clear the area Nurse Baker, Nurse Chapple... Please...

LIZZIE: (*trying to revive him*) Come on, Robby/...

ELLA: Lizzie –

LIZZIE: Come on/...

ELLA: Matron needs to tend to him.

LIZZIE: (*distressed*) It must be the tablets...

ENID: Nurse Baker, please...

Lizzie stands back. Enid bends over Robby as the audience are ushered away by Ella.

ELLA: If you could all move to one side. I'm afraid this is a medical emergency. Just over there if you would. That's right. Thank you.

LIZZIE: (*distressed, shouts at the audience*) Give the
                poor man his privacy!

ENID: Nurse Baker, could you telephone for an
                ambulance please. (*beat*) Nurse Baker!
                An ambulance.

LIZZIE: Yes, Matron... (*she runs towards the house*)

ELLA: (*ushering people away*) Could you move
                along, now – over there if you would...
                That's right...

SCENE 12.

Location: Rose Garden, travelling towards the rose bushes.

*Hatfeild is a little shaken, but nevertheless tries to play the
host.*

HATFEILD: (*direct address*) Well... er... as you can see,
                we're now standing in the er... Rose
                Garden... in front of Morden Cottage...
                (*gesturing for the audience to move away
                from the incident*) Move a little further this
                way, if you would, to allow more space for
                the nurses to... erm... Yes, that's right....

Thank you… Thank you… (*beat*) Of course, we didn't have roses here during the War. The land had far more practical demands to fulfil – such as feeding our convalescing soldiers. But we planted roses here in the early 1920s. And very beautiful they are too, especially in the height of summer when all the flowers are in full bloom. Though sadly at this time of year, most of the petals have er… fallen… (*he clears his throat, regaining his composure*) Sometimes one needs to let the beds rest for a while to… recover, as it were, from their ordeal… Here you can see dahlias have been planted to replenish the soil, making it ready for action again. And it really is most gratifying to see new buds appear each year and know they've made it through another winter. They need care, of course. But luckily we've plenty of volunteers at Morden Hall to help with that. And I pitch in and do whatever I can. I'm what you might call an enthusiastic amateur.

<u>SCENE 13.</u>

Location: Rose Garden, amongst the rose bushes.

Hatfeild is tending his flowers: dead-heading, spraying, supporting the larger blooms with stakes. Billy enters. As he approaches Hatfeild, he appraises one or two flowers.

BILLY: Nice day for it, Squire.

HATFEILD: Not bad.

BILLY: Me mum's birthday Sunday.

HATFEILD: You celebrating?

BILLY: Nothing special. You know how it is.
                What with the War an' that. But what
                me mum always says is... So long as I've
                got me health and me family then I can't
                be wanting for much.

HATFEILD: Absolutely. Good for her.

A pause as Billy considers his strategy.

BILLY: But to my mind, sir, she deserves a bit of a
                treat. D'you know what I'm saying?

HATFEILD: You'd like some flowers for your mother.

BILLY: Oooh, no sir. I wouldn't be so bold.

Hatfeild offers Billy his secateurs.

HATFEILD: Here. Why don't you cut some of these?
                Go on, son. What else are they for, eh?

Billy takes the secateurs and gives a little nod of appreciation.

BILLY: Aw, much obliged to you, Squire. She'll
                be cock a hoop.

HATFEILD: Just pop the secateurs back in the tree
                when you've finished.

BILLY: I will. Would that be the usual tree, sir?

HATFEILD: Usual tree, Billy. Thank you.

Hatfeild slips to the back of the audience as Billy begins to cut some flowers. Lizzie appears and is clearly outraged by what she sees.

LIZZIE: Billy? Billy! What the heck d'you think you're doin'?

BILLY: No, cos… He gimme permission. (*glancing round, he realises Hatfeild has disappeared*) No, he did though. I told him it's me Mum's birthday Sunday and he says I'm to help meself.

LIZZIE: I can check..?

BILLY: On me life. I swear.

Lizzie can't help but admire the flowers.

LIZZIE: You better not be lying.

BILLY: Cross me heart.

Billy crosses his heart and cuts a few more blooms.

BILLY: You heard anything about that soldier?

LIZZIE: What?

BILLY: The one what what went all womicky.

LIZZIE: Oh, Robby. Yes. He's going to be all right.

BILLY: Well, that's all that matters then, innit? Sis?

LIZZIE: Yeah, maybe.

She gazes around.

LIZZIE: Nice 'ere. Quiet.

BILLY: Too quiet if you ask me.

She touches one of the flowers.

BILLY: Chrysanths.

He gives Lizzie a flower and she inhales its scent.

LIZZIE: Funny smell off of 'em.

Billy looks a little crestfallen.

LIZZIE: She'll love 'em, Billy.

He beams. She smiles back.

LIZZIE: She'll love 'em

Billy cuts one or two more flowers then heads off to put the secateurs in Hatfeild's favourite hiding place. Lizzie wanders around admiring the garden. Alex approaches. He hesitates a couple of times, glancing over his shoulder before he speaks.

ALEX: Nurse Baker..? (*he clears his throat, then speaks louder*) Lizzie…

LIZZIE: (*beaming*) Hello. What's up? Ella said he was all right. He is all right. Isn't he?

ALEX: Robby's fine.

LIZZIE: Oh, thank God. Thought you was gonna
                 tell me... I dunno. Something awful.

Alex makes several futile attempts to interrupt Lizzie's flow.

LIZZIE: I did tell her, you know. Matron. I says
                 them tablets aren't agreeing with him.
                 Could see meself something weren't right.
                 And even though Ella keeps tellin' me it's
                 not my fault, it's me what give him 'em,
                 innit? In the end. 'An fair enough so
                 everyone makes mistakes but I'd sooner it
                 wasn't me, that's all. Can't afford to, can
                 ya? Make a mistake. Cos the truth is
                 people...

Alex fixes Lizzie with a steady gaze. Her voice cracks.

LIZZIE: People might die.

He takes his cap off.

LIZZIE: Don't.

ALEX: Your mum...

LIZZIE: Don't tell me. Don't tell me nothing bad.
                 Please?

ALEX: She... She needs you, Lizzie.

LIZZIE: Jack..?

ALEX: She needs you.

Lizzie drops Billy's flower and flees to her mother. Alex picks up the flower. Beat.

ALEX: Must be her bro' was it.

HATFEILD: Yes. Her brother Jack.

SCENE 14.

Location: in front of Morden Cottage.

Hatfeild takes a pear out of his pocket and considers it then drops it back in his pocket. Alex and Hatfeild move across to a patch of wilted plants during the following.

ALEX: Those lilies aren't doing very well.

HATFEILD: Too much water maybe...

68

ALEX: You could be right. Perhaps – if I may –
            (*adjusting the plant*) here – and here. Ah –
            jus' the thing… (*he sees a twig, props up
            the plant with it*)

HATFEILD: You have a gift.

ALEX: It no gift - I work on the land all me life.

HATFEILD: Sugar?

ALEX: Yeah that, an' a few crops for my mother
            and brothers. (*indicating the hoe*) May I?

HATFEILD: Is it part of your regime?

ALEX: Nah, I've done me prescribed time hoeing
            for today.

HATFEILD: Well, I won't tell if you won't.

They smile. The two men hoe together.

ALEX: They say you were in Virginia?

HATFEILD: Yes, for many years before my father died.

ALEX: What's it like there – for men such as me, I
            mean?

HATFEILD: Not so bad as it was.

ALEX: We will be a better world – when all this is
            over.

HATFEILD: I hope so.

They continue to hoe together. In the distance Lizzie speaks to Billy. We cannot hear their conversation – except a cry of pain from Billy, who is distraught and runs away. Lizzie calls after him. Alex and Hatfeild glance up at them then continue hoeing.

HATFEILD: Were you shot at the Front, son?

ALEX: Nah. King George's Steam Engine.

HATFEILD: What's that?

ALEX: Is what they call us – on account we build the roads and railways. (*pointing at his pelvis*) Crushed – unloadin' a shell.

HATFEILD: I see.

ALEX: It's nat all a blaze of glory ya know.

HATFEILD: No. (*beat*) Will you go back to the Front do you think?

ALEX: Not now. They only take the able bodied men.

They continue to hoe.

HATFEILD: Do you like it here, Sergeant Forbes? At Morden Hall I mean.

ALEX: Very much. Especially the tea – the tea is always excellent in England.

HATFEILD: It is.

ALEX: And I've never eaten so well in all my life
             – so many eggs and creams and radishes.

HATFEILD: I wonder - would you like a job?

ALEX: A job, sir?

HATFEILD: Here in the Park. In the garden. You've a
             talent for it.

ALEX: Ah, it's temptin', that's for sure... But
             there's so much to do back home, ya see.
             Thank you for the offer though.

HATFEILD: You'll go back to the Caribbean then?

ALEX: Soon as I'm fit for the trip. Men like me
             who fought for King and Empire, we will
             build the new Jamaica.

HATFEILD: And 'tread the road to glory'?

ALEX: Ah yeah... It is all possible now. This war
             has taught me that.

HATFEILD: Well, I wish you luck, Sergeant.

ALEX: Thank you. (*beat*) Now - must be time for
             grub, eh, is it?

HATFEILD: (*glances at his pocket watch*) Gracious..!
             You'd better not be late. I know how
             Matron likes to keep a tight ship.

ALEX: (*he laughs*) Indeed she does. (*beat*) Thank
             you, Squire.

71

Hatfeild nods. Alex exits.

<u>SCENE 15.</u>

Location: path beside the Rose Garden.

Enid is marching along with Ella chasing after her.

ELLA: What *are* you?

ENID: I beg your pardon?

ELLA: Well, you're not human. Her brother died.

ENID: I'm well aware of the fact. Thank you.

ELLA: The fact? The… Jesus, I just don't
            believe you.

ENID: I'd sooner you didn't blaspheme. In fact,
            I'd have thought as a Presbyterian…

ELLA: Bugger that.

ENID: I find profanity equally offensive.

ELLA: D'you know what I find offensive?

Enid makes as if to utter.

ELLA: The way you're treating Lizzie. She's a
            brilliant nurse. Why can't you see that?

ENID: You're emotional.

ELLA: Yes. Yes, I am. Because I'm human.

ENID: Well, there's nothing exceptional about
            that.

ELLA: I mean I can actually feel Lizzie's pain?

ENID: In our profession, Nurse Chapple, it's
            prudent to retain a little distance.

ELLA: Her brother just died.

Enid averts her gaze.

ELLA: You haven't got a clue, have you?

Enid looks back at Ella.

ENID: We can't afford to be sentimental.

ELLA:　　　　　　What is *wrong* with you?

ENID:　　　　　　There's nothing wrong with me, Nurse
　　　　　　　　Chapple. And might I remind you, you're
　　　　　　　　still on probation. You'd do well to use a
　　　　　　　　little restraint.

Ella struggles to compose herself.

ELLA:　　　　　　I pity you. I do. You clearly have no idea
　　　　　　　　what a family actually means. You're
　　　　　　　　married to your work, aren't you? And
　　　　　　　　nothing else matters. She's devastated.
　　　　　　　　Her whole world just fell apart. And
　　　　　　　　you... God! And she didn't abandon her
　　　　　　　　duty. How dare you accuse her of that.

ENID:　　　　　　She left work without my permission.

ELLA:　　　　　　She took her mother home.

ENID:　　　　　　She should not have left the premises
　　　　　　　　without my permission. Whatever the
　　　　　　　　circumstances.

ELLA:　　　　　　Her mother collapsed. Did you know
　　　　　　　　that? She couldn't breathe.

ENID:　　　　　　Hysteria.

ELLA:　　　　　　Jesus Christ!

Pause.

ENID:	Three men were left without adequate supervision.
ELLA:	So, the rest of us rallied. They were fine.
ENID:	I had to make a stand.
ELLA:	Using Lizzie as an example.
ENID:	That really wasn't my intention.
ELLA:	She'd have been a liability in any case. She couldn't possibly have done any work.
ENID:	Protocol must be adhered to.
ELLA:	So you bawled her out. I mean, Christ! In the circumstances?
ENID:	I simply reminded Nurse Baker that she needs to inform me in the future. I can't have staff just swanning off.
ELLA:	Swanning off!
ENID:	Besides, some people find it a comfort. Routine. Normality.
ELLA:	Normality? What would you know about normal?

Pause.

ELLA:	The day I started here, you said... I remember this. I distinctly remember this. You told me that you deal with human

beings, not machines. But, you know what? You're not human, Matron Woods. You're not a human being. You're a machine.

Ella stalks off leaving Enid alone with her thoughts. Noticing Enid's distress, Hatfeild coughs to attract the audience's attention.

HATFEILD: (*direct address, in a tactful whisper*) If you wouldn't mind... I think perhaps you should come with me... (*he gestures*)

As the audience follow, Hatfeild catches sight of Billy ahead of him hacking at the plants.

HATFEILD: Oh, dear! We'd better hurry... (*he hurries off to prevent Billy doing more damage*)

SCENE 16.

Location: patch of ground next to the gazebo.

Billy is hacking at the plants with a spade, tears and snot streaming down his face, when Hatfeild arrives.

BILLY: Bleedin', bleedin'/bugger!

HATFEILD: Steady son – steady – (*he gently takes the rake from him*)

Billy bursts into tears.

HATFEILD: Now, now, son, come on. Your brother
            wouldn't want this...

BILLY: He was a hero. Our Jack was a hero... (*he
            picks up a trowel and stabs at some flowers*)

Hatfeild watches uneasily.

HATFEILD: Yes. Yes, he was... (*he prises the trowel
            from Billy's hand*)

BILLY: It's that bleedin' bugger — pardon me, sir —
            but the Recruiting Sergeant — he give me a
            mouth full/...

HATFEILD: You've not tried to join up?

BILLY: He wouldn't take me, sir, the bleedin'
            bugger. He wouldn't take me. And now
            Jerry will live — Jerry will live who killed
            our Jack. (*he stabs at a plant with a stick*)

HATFEILD: Steady, son. It's not the marigold's fault.
            (*he takes the stick from Billy*)

BILLY: But I can't just sit here and do nothing.

HATFEILD: You're only fifteen, Billy. You're a child.

BILLY: I'm old enough. I can fire a gun. Our Jack
            let me fire one when he was home on leave.

HATFEILD: How would it be for your mother and
            sisters if you left them all alone? You're

the man of the house now. You have to look after them.

Billy continues to cry and mutter 'bleedin' bugger', occasionally stabbing at the plants. Hatfeild watches him anxiously.

HATFEILD: Listen, Billy - I've a job for a man — if you'll take it on.

BILLY: (*wiping his dirty tear-streaked face*) Tell me, Squire. I can do it.

HATFEILD: I've been having a problem with the rats from the Wandle. One rat in particular — big fellow — long tail — nasty sharp teeth. Comes out from the river and eats the veggies.

BILLY: He's a pest that one and no mistake.

HATFEILD: I don't want our soldiers to go without — so I need a brave young man like you to help me with the task.

BILLY: Don't worry, Squire, I'm your man... (*he picks up a spade and swings it around*)

HATFEILD: Careful there, son —

BILLY: I'm gonna go and kill that rat. /Aaaaaaaaaaaaaaagh! (*he runs off swinging the spade wildly and screaming*

savagely) Gonna kill the rat —
aaaaaaaaaaaaaagh!

HATFEILD: (calls) Billy — come back! Mind those...
No, that's not... Oh, dear!

Hatfeild watches Billy go. He sighs.

HATFEILD: (direct address to the audience) Well —
onwards...

Hatfeild leads the audience to where Lizzie sits waiting for Enid.

SCENE 17.

Location: gazebo.

Lizzie is waiting for Enid. Enid enters. She goes to the desk and sits down. Lizzie glances up at her.

ENID: Nurse Baker.

LIZZIE: I'm sorry, Matron.

ENID: Apology accepted.

LIZZIE: Thank you.

ENID: I   think,   perhaps,   under   the
                circumstances/...

LIZZIE: My mum...

Enid gives a little nod.

ENID: It's difficult for you.   I can appreciate
      that.

LIZZIE: Thank you. I didn't know what to do. Me
                head couldn't think right, you know? So I
                just... I just done what I felt. I know it
                was wrong now.   But all I could think
                about was getting her home. Keeping her
                safe. Helping her. I'm sorry.

Lizzie takes a shuddering breath.

LIZZIE: Couldn't be no help to her anyhow.
                Weren't nothing I could do for her. Just...
                Being there, you know. Holding her hand.
                Stroking her face. Telling her... Telling
                her she wasn't gonna die. She couldn't
                'cos how... What would that do to Billy?

She gives a little hiccup.

LIZZIE: He... Billy. He loved Jack an' all.
             Thought the sun shone out his...

She glances at Enid.

ENID: Backside.

LIZZIE: Yeah. He was. He was...

She groans in exasperation at her persistent tears.

LIZZIE: Can't stop...

*She wipes fiercely at her eyes with her hands. Enid takes out
her hanky and passes it to Lizzie.*

ENID: Here.

LIZZIE: Thank you. Wish I could just...

She stamps her foot.

LIZZIE: ...Stop crying.

She struggles to compose herself.

LIZZIE: He was the big one.

ENID: Older than you?

LIZZIE: Younger than me but older than Billy.
             Billy's the little one. Jack's...

She shrugs.

ENID: How old was Jack?

LIZZIE: Seventeen.

A long pause.

LIZZIE: Can't... Can't believe I won't see him no more. Hear him.

She giggles as she fights her tears.

LIZZIE: He always done this thing when he come in the door of a night-time. 'I'm home, Mum and hungry enough to devour an 'orse.' And he'd make this...

She glances at Enid.

LIZZIE: ...coarse sound like a cow gnawing a turnip.

Enid looks quizzically at Lizzie. Lizzie shakes her head.

LIZZIE: I can't do it. The... You know. The sound.

ENID: Well. Never mind.

LIZZIE: 'Un then... 'Anyone in?' he'd go. 'I'm...'

Her voice cracks.

LIZZIE: 'I'm home.'

She surrenders to her tears for a moment or two. Enid makes as if to touch her but refrains.

LIZZIE: 'Un then, Mum... Daft really. 'Go on with you' she'd say. 'Slice of cold tongue 'll have to do you cos I'm all out of horses

today.' 'Un they'd laugh, pair of 'em.
Silly devils. Every single night I miss him,
Matron. I really do.

Enid averts her gaze for a moment.

ENID: Well. You'll learn to accept it.

*Lizzie twists her hanky, glances at Enid then looks away. She
shrugs.*

LIZZIE: It's like I say... Me Mum, you know?
                 She's took it really bad. Worser 'un me
                 even. Well, it's...

*She sniffs, wipes her nose on her hand, glances at Enid and
wipes her hand on her clothes.*

ENID: Use the hanky.

LIZZIE: Stupid. Sorry.

*Lizzie wipes her nose with the hanky. She looks in the hanky
and catches Enid's eye.*

LIZZIE: Sorry.

Enid dismisses Lizzie's concern with a little shake of her head.

LIZZIE: When she got the word... Me Mum.
                 She... This... This sound. I've never
                 heard her make that noise before. Sounds
                 like... No word of a lie, Matron, but it
                 sounded like she'd swallowed a bear. This

kind of roar in her throat? You (*she hiccups*) know?

LIZZIE: She said it feels like her heart's been ripped out her chest. Being a Mum, innit? Not that you'd know.

ENID: No.

A long pause.

LIZZIE: It's my fault, you know?

ENID: Don't be ridiculous.

LIZZIE: No, it is though. Wouldn't never of joined up if it wasn't for me. Stuff I said to 'em. Our Billy and... Jack. Billy's me kid brother. He's...

ENID: I know who Billy is.

LIZZIE: You... Yeah. Course. You would do.

She sniffs, makes as if to wipe her nose with her hand and remembers to use the hanky.

LIZZIE: Stuff I told 'em. 'Bout soldiers an' that. How every... How every girl loves a soldier because they're brave and dashing and strong. I'm not though. I'm not strong. I'm a stupid, feeble girl with a big gob and no brains.

ENID: You mustn't blame yourself.

84

LIZZIE: But I do.

ENID: It's self-indulgent nonsense and it does no
            one any favours.

LIZZIE: S'pose.

ENID: Young men sign up for all kinds of reasons.
            A bit of adventure's what most of them
            want. Friendship. Good food. To escape
            trouble..?

LIZZIE: Not Jack. He never done nothing bad.

ENID: Well. Good.

A pause as they both reflect on Jack's conduct for a moment.

LIZZIE: All right, so he weren't no angel but...

*She begins to compose herself. She sniffs, wipes her nose with
the hanky.*

LIZZIE: Well, it weren't nothing much in the
            scheme of things. Just...

She shrugs.

LIZZIE: The odd bit of cheese. Couple of seed
            packets. A pencil. And some...

ENID: Right. Well then.

Enid cocks her head. Lizzie takes a shuddering breath.

LIZZIE: S'pose. Yeah. P'raps it weren't nothing
            to do with me.

ENID: I very much doubt that it was. Now, go
               and wash your face.

Lizzie makes as if to leave.

ENID: And Nurse Baker? I don't want to see you
               here before the middle of next week.
               You're quite unfit for work.

LIZZIE: Thank you. I mean thank you, Matron.

ENID: Good bye.

*Lizzie exits. Enid is struggling to compose herself. A long
pause before Hatfeild begins to make his way to the front of the
audience.*

ENID: (*to herself, her voice cracking*) This ghastly
               war.

*Glancing up, Enid notices Hatfeild. She shakes her head and
wipes her nose with her hanky.*

ENID: Fine. I'm …

She looks up at him. Nods.

ENID: Really.

He holds her gaze for a moment.

HATFEILD: Good. That's… Good.

She looks away. Beat.

 HATFEILD: Poor Lizzie.

86

ENID: She'll cope.

HATFEILD: Yes, I daresay she will.

ENID: Well, there isn't very much of a choice, is there?

He's a little taken aback by the intensity of her delivery. Enid looks away for a moment.

HATFEILD: Damn difficult business.

ENID: Yes.

HATFEILD: If there's anything I...

He shakes his head.

HATFEILD: Damned fool.

Enid glances at Hatfeild.

HATFEILD: Me. I just... (*he shrugs*) Helpless, aren't we?

Enid smiles.

ENID: I appreciate your concern.

He holds her gaze for a moment then is suddenly very aware of himself.

HATFEILD: Nights are drawing in.

ENID: Yes. Our summer's gone.

HATFEID: So it would seem.

87

Hatfeild gives a little nod and leaves.   Enid watches him disappear. Enid addresses the audience.

ENID: If you'd all excuse me.

Enid exits.

Location: café garden.

*Early evening. Enid is sitting in the garden feeding the birds.
Ella approaches and is a little taken aback by Enid's apparent
delight in the birds. Clocking Ella, Enid stuffs the bag in her
pocket and brushes crumbs off her skirt.*

ELLA: Don't mind me.

ENID: They fascinate me. Birds. My father was
              an ornithologist. We used to spend hours
              together in the garden.

ELLA: I was a daddy's girl. My Mom says.

An awkward silence.

ELLA: Everyone knows about the service now.

ENID: Good.

ELLA: The stable yard. Seven thirty. All the
              men are going. Well, there's just the odd
              one or two of course. But I promised them
              an order of service.   We can read it
              through to them after.

ENID: He was pretty popular.

ELLA: I think, perhaps... Well, for the men at
              least, it's Lizzie. They're going for her.

Enid gives a little nod of acknowledgment.

ELLA: She's devastated. I don't think she'll ever
               get over it.

ENID: She's not the only one to have lost
               someone.

Ella stares at Enid. Enid averts her gaze.

ELLA: You've really got it in for her, haven't
               you? You've always had it in for her.
               Why?

ENID: I haven't got it in for her. I haven't got it
               in for anyone. Why on earth would I?

ELLA: You tell me.

A long pause.

ELLA: He could've died. Robby Stephens? He
               could've died.

ENID: I'm well aware of that.

ELLA: And Lizzie was the one who had to deal
               with it. See him like that. It was horrible.
               Terrifying. She thought... She thought he
               was dying. That she'd... She thought he
               was dying.

ENID: She's very sensitive.

ELLA: She cares.

ENID: Of course she does.

ELLA: Because it's our duty to care.

ENID: It *is* our duty... And we do.

ELLA: No. Lizzie *really* cares.   And   thank
               goodness someone does.

Enid turns away from Ella and gazes up at the trees.

ELLA: What about Billy?

ENID: He'll learn to live with it. But he'll need
               time. They all will.

ELLA: They grew up together. Lizzie and Jack.
               He was one of the few people in the world
               she could completely trust. She adored
               him.

ENID: I know.

ELLA: No. You don't. You've got no idea.

A long pause.

ENID: I've got a brother.

ELLA: You have?

ENID: He died last year.

ELLA: This... This war.

ENID: It wasn't the War that killed him. Not
               exactly. He didn't fight. He couldn't. He
               was beaten to death in the street.

Ella glances uncertainly at Enid.

ELLA: I'm… I'm so sorry. I… I didn't know.

ENID: No one knows.

ELLA: How…   If you don't mind my asking?
               How old was he?

ENID: Twenty six.

ELLA: A little brother.

Enid gives a tiny nod.

ELLA: I've… Jean is… She's my little sister.
               Miles younger than me.

ENID: How old is she?

ELLA: Fourteen.

Enid gazes at Ella. She nods.

ELLA: What… What was his name? Your/…

ENID: My little brother? David.

ELLA: A conscientious objector.

ENID: No. Flat feet.

ELLA: I can't imagine…

ENID: No.

A long pause.

ELLA: I guess we all make mistakes.

ENID: Yes.

ELLA: It's human.

Enid looks at Ella. Ella holds her gaze. Enid looks away.

ENID: I haven't forgiven myself.

ELLA: Robby Stephens?

ENID: I should've listened. There's no excuse.

ELLA: Not even if you're bone tired, emotionally drained…

ENID: I was bloody minded.

ELLA: You see stuff differently, that's all.

ENID: I'm almost twice your age.

ELLA: So?

ENID: You're both very (*beat*) passionate. About your work I mean.

ELLA: I guess that's because it's all new.

ENID: Exactly.

A pause.

ENID: It's   impressive.   Your   dedication. Enthusiasm. Your expertise.

ELLA: We still… Lizzie and me. We still (*beat*)
               have a lot to learn.

*Ella meets Enid's eye. She holds her gaze for a moment. Enid
gives a tiny nod of acknowledgment.*

ENID: She's a good nurse.

ELLA: Lizzie?

ENID: Instinctive.

ELLA: She cares.

*Enid nods. She is close to tears. Ella doesn't know quite what
to do or say.*

ENID: It's just…   I'm a little over-tired I
               suppose.

ELLA: What else would you do?

ENID: There is nothing else.

Pause.

ENID: This bloody carnage.

ELLA: I have nightmares every night.

ENID: I used to.

ELLA: You learn to deal with it. I guess.

ENID: You have to. But I'm thinking about the
               future. I don't want to die alone.

ELLA: You're not sick, are you?

ENID: I'm... No. I'm not sick.

Enid gazes into the distance for a moment.

ELLA: She really looks up to you. You know?
                 When she first arrived all she ever wanted
                 was to fall in love. Become a wife and
                 mother. But then being here. That's all
                 changed. She wants to be a nurse now.
                 She wants to be like you.

ENID: It's a noble ambition.

Ella beams.

ELLA: That's what I said.

ENID: Motherhood.

Ella is taken aback.

ELLA: You don't want to have babies. God!
                 Seriously?

ENID: I don't know what I want. Not anymore.
                 All this.

ELLA: The War?

ENID: It's changed me. One little boy in
                 particular.

ELLA: Who?

ENID: Not here. In France.

ELLA: Tell me. Please?

ENID: He was fourteen. Gas attack. Pneumonia. His mother couldn't be there so I sat with him night and day. Held his hand. Talked to him. Listened. One night, not long before he died he reached out his hand. Blindly, searching. Frantic. I caught hold of his hand and held it tight, told him he was safe and that I... I wouldn't leave him. Then he whispered something I couldn't quite hear. So I leaned in close. I do love you, he said. Will you kiss me?

ELLA: You kissed him?

ENID: He was like a son to me. How I imagine it might be. And yes, I did I kissed him. Once for his mother.

Her voice cracks.

ENID: And then for me.

Enid wipes away a tear. Ella offers Enid her hanky. Enid takes it and wipes her eyes.

ELLA: That's... Well that's nursing for you. (*she shrugs*) I guess.

ENID: Yes.

Enid smiles at Ella.

ELLA: I remember what you said when I came
          here.

ENID: About machines?

ELLA: About people. You said, it's only when
          you've worked with someone that you can
          know their true worth.

ENID: Did I/...

ELLA: I agree.

ENID: It seems a long time ago now.

*She straightens Ella's headdress. Ella holds her gaze for a
moment. Enid looks away.*

ENID: Well. This won't get the men their tea.
          Off you go, Nurse Chapple. Make haste.

*Ella exits. Enid gazes after her for a moment or two. Billy,
meanwhile, is tearing back from the river with a dead rat,
whistling 'It's a Long Way to Tipperary'. His drum hangs
loosely around his neck. He runs up to Enid swinging the rat
by the tail.*

BILLY: Got him, Matron. Smack on top the 'ead
          with the spade. Dead.

Enid recoils. Billy chucks the rat into the river.

ENID: Your brother would be proud.

Billy beams.

BILLY: You gonna come an' all, are you?

ENID: I'm sorry..?

BILLY: This special service.

ENID: Of course.

BILLY: Right. Good.

Enid smiles.

BILLY: Best get off then. You tell the others then,
            would ya?

ENID: Yes, fine. Off you go. I can see to our
            guests.

She turns to address the audience.

ENID: Well, if you'd all like to follow me..?

Billy spins around and calls back over his shoulder.

BILLY: You wanna get a move on. There's some
            what's already 'ere.

*The audience follows Billy. Enid soberly brings up the rear.
Hatfeild stands waiting to lead the audience back into the
stable yard the way they first came.*

BILLY: (*quietening the audience*) Sssh! Can we
            'ave a bit of quiet now please?

*Billy bangs the drum solemnly. Hatfeild opens the doors and
leads the audience inside.*

<u>SCENE 19.</u>

Location: stable yard.

Hatfeild stands on a raised platform surrounded by the cast. Morden's Roll of Honour is displayed.

HATFEILD: Thank you all for coming here today to remember Jack Arnold Baker. As you know, Jack was killed in action on the 12th of September 1916. He was seventeen. Beloved son, brother, sweetheart and friend, we all knew and loved him. Warm, witty, kind and devoted to his family, I can say with heartfelt conviction that Jack was one of my favourite employees and he'll be deeply missed both as a colleague and a friend. We know how he lived and we know how we died. But as we gather here to remember Jack, let us all spare a moment to remember the soldier we didn't know. The soldier whose name, rank and number lies in an unmarked place in a field a long, long way from home.

The audience is invited to light a small candle (tea light) in memory of all those who fell in the Great War, perhaps commemorating the dead from their own families while the eulogies continue:

ELLA: We remember also Elizabeth Ewing Chapple. Ella served as a V.A.D. at Morden Hall until the end of the War. After travelling the world she met and married Eric Bodington. They had no children.   Ella died in Hove in 1971, leaving her estate to her little sister Jean.

ENID: Matron Enid Woods remained dedicated to her profession until she retired from nursing in 1937.   She never married and lived alone in the Orkneys where she died in 1967 after spending the last years of her life running a sanctuary for injured birds.

ALEX: Sergeant Alex Forbes of the Third Battalion of the British West India Regiment returned to Jamaica after convalescence and became an active member of the People's National Party. He farmed the land – and still enjoyed knitting – until his death in 1964 – just two years after Jamaica achieved independence.

ROBBY: Private Robby Stephens never returned to military action. After convalescing at Morden Hall for shell shock he received the Silver War Badge for honourable discharge and became a bank clerk. He remained unmarried, taking early retirement in 1955. He died shortly afterwards.

LIZZIE: Lizzie Baker served as a V.A.D. for two years at Morden Hall before she met and married Corporal Walter Williams on the 27th April 1918. They had three sons – Arnold, Billy and Walter. Their eldest, Flying Officer Arnold John Williams died on the 15th September 1940. His mother, Lizzie, died the following spring.

BILLY: Lizzie's little brother, Billy Baker, achieved his ambition of becoming a soldier, eventually convincing the Recruiting Officer that he was old enough to fight. He died in action at Passchendaele in July 1917, just 2 days before his sixteenth birthday.

HATFEILD: Gilliat Edward Hatfeild died on 9th February 1941 at the age of 76. His coffin was carried on a hay cart to its burial place at St Lawrence Church, Morden, followed by crowds of mourners. In his will he left Morden Hall and Park in the care of the National Trust to be used in perpetuity by the local community. He remains faithful to his trust.

The End.